M000290934

Where's the Wisdom in Service-Learning?

Where's the Wisdom in Service-Learning?

edited by

Robert Shumer

University of Minnesota (retired)
Metropolitan State University

INFORMATION AGE PUBLISHING, INC.
Charlotte, NC • www.infoagepub.com

Library of Congress Cataloging-in-Publication Data

A CIP record for this book is available from the Library of Congress
http://www.loc.gov

ISBN: 978-1-68123-864-7 (Paperback)
        978-1-68123-865-4 (Hardcover)
        978-1-68123-866-1 (ebook)

Copyright © 2017 Information Age Publishing Inc.

All rights reserved. No part of this publication may be reproduced, stored in a
retrieval system, or transmitted, in any form or by any means, electronic, mechanical,
photocopying, microfilming, recording or otherwise, without written permission
from the publisher.

Printed in the United States of America

CONTENTS

v

PURPOSE OF THE BOOK

The purpose of this book is to capture the wisdom of those involved in the service-learning movement who have helped to shape its foundation, formation, and development. The book was inspired by the realization that many of us are getting a lot older and that our ability to live, to share, and to interact is diminishing and/or declining. While I am now 70 years old, our oldest contributor is 95. Everyone else is in their 50s, 60s, 70s, or 80s, and still actively continuing their life-long work.

The book is dedicated to those who have contributed so much to the field and the world and are no longer with us, except in spirit. To Diane Hedin, Joan Shine, Judy Rauner, Rahima Wade, Lynn Montrose, and to many others who have shaped our service-learning enterprise, we say thank you and want you to know you are not forgotten . . . and very much appreciated. We hope this contribution can rise to the level of your work and inspire young people to continue the cause.

It is the hope of these collective authors that the understandings shared through our chapters will illustrate and illuminate where the field started, where it went, and where it might continue to thrive. While the first book to address the modern beginnings, *Service-Learning: A Movement's Pioneers Reflect on Its Origins, Practice, and Future* (Stanton, Giles, & Cruz, 1999) attempted to capture the impressions from early adopters of how and why the movement started, this volume is focused on sharing the collective knowledge and wisdom of some of the early people involved in developing programs and connections that placed service learning where it is today.

Authors were asked to reflect on their lives and to capture the high and low points of the movement and to make recommendations for future

Where's the Wisdom in Service-Learning?, pages vii–viii
Copyright © 2017 by Information Age Publishing
All rights of reproduction in any form reserved.

participants to apply this wisdom to ensure that service learning is a viable program and a thriving initiative that will continue to accomplish its goals of social change and community improvement. While this was the charge of the book, most authors decided to express their interpretations of the strengths and weaknesses through personal stories of their lifelong involvement in engaging in service-learning actions or activities....or what we think of as service learning even when the term wasn't established when they were doing "it."

The value of the book will be known when, and if, young leaders find and use this wisdom to make improvements in the quality and quantity of programs that are labeled as "service learning." It is our hope that the contributions of "wise" older folks will have an effect and impact on those who are responsible for continuing the movement.

—**Robert Shumer**

FOREWORD

This book arrives on the scene at an important moment in the evolution of service-learning pedagogy. Fifty years ago, as described in chapters six and seven, Bill Ramsay and Bob Sigmon coined the term to describe their effort to establish a "Manpower Development Program" at the Oak Ridge Institute of Nuclear Studies in eastern Tennessee. Their goal was to recruit and enable university students from the southern region of the United States to join their effort to build the capacity of local residents to qualify for employment at the lab. They sought a term that would describe the actions these students could take and to point out that they intended these experiences to be educational and growth producing for the students as well as ones of charitable giving of their time and skills.

> We were trying to find a phrase that would describe the program, and we tried all kinds of things—experiential learning, experience learning, work learning, action learning, all these different things. We decided to call it service learning, because service implied a value consideration that none of the other words that we came up with did.... It was more of an attitude, more of an approach to be of service.... You could have experience with the Mafia and it would be tremendous learning perhaps, but it's not the kind of thing we were talking about. We were looking for something with a value connotation.... It had to be real service, not academics, not made up, not superficial, not tangential, but real. (Stanton, Giles, & Cruz, p. 67)

In encouraging and enabling the contributing authors to tell their stories from these 50 years and share the wisdom they gained through their

Where's the Wisdom in Service-Learning?, pages ix–xiii
Copyright © 2017 by Information Age Publishing
All rights of reproduction in any form reserved.

reflections, editor Shumer provides our field with a valuable opportunity to step back and reflect on where we came from, where we have come, and perhaps where we are going or ought to go.

The book's authors ruminate over three sets of wisdoms: those related to reflection on the field's early days; those related to its extraordinary development over these 50 years; and those related considering the field's future within a broader movement now labeled "community engaged learning" or "civic or community engagement."

A central feature of the wisdom shared by the authors gained from their early days came through their struggles to establish, develop, and maintain their programs and positions within typically hostile university or school environments. Service-learning wasn't exactly new 50 years ago. It's roots reach back to the land grant legislation of the 1860s that spawned university extension programs, to John Dewey's pragmatism of the early years of the last century and its expression in laboratory schools and settlement houses, etc. (Sigmon, 1995). However, something snapped in the 1960s in the culture of young people, a snap that stretched from politics to popular music. All of a sudden young people wanted to and were encouraged to explore their communities and the wider world through volunteerism, VISTA, Peace Corps. As described by some of the book's authors, who came of age during those tumultuous times of civil rights and anti-Vietnam war movements, many of them carried this yearning for social change into educational settings where they could experiment with new forms of more active, critical experiential education designed to encourage civic activism on the part of students and tangible benefit to communities. However, everyone tinkering with this work in those early days had to come to terms with the assets and liabilities connected to their marginal status as newcomers practicing an innovative, but suspect approach to teaching and learning and to partnering higher education institutions used to an "ivory tower" existence to the "disorderly chaos" of communities. Readers should sift through these chapters to identify and reflect on what these early practitioners learned about institutional marginality, especially now that service-learning practice finds itself in much safer, more central positions in the academy with identifiable professional roles, when dialogue seems to have shifted from marginality to discussion of how to establish graduate professional certification programs.

Moving chronologically forward, readers will find a set of ruminations in these chapters, which are animated by critical reflection on the hard work of establishing and maintaining programs and positions within institutions and building a field. At this stage, authors highlight wisdom gained from their success at this work, as well as the challenges that came with it. Many comment on dual roles they found themselves in. On the one hand they were strongly focused internally, building their programs from marginal beachheads into core academic programs, with some asking what is gained and what may be lost when a field solidifies itself, expands and matures. On the other hand, some of these same authors speak of the efforts they made in wider field building through national organizations such as NSIEE and Campus Compact, which became key support bases providing form for professional exchange, mutual support, and opportunities for research and publication. Some speak of this work at the field level as movement building, while their campus work resembled infiltration.

Many authors conclude their chapters wondering about what has been accomplished and where the field may go or should go in the future. Here a central concern is a perception that practitioners and researchers, having now achieved status and position within schools and the academy, appear more concerned with students' development than with the needs, issues, and challenges of the communities in which their students work. Has the field, perhaps unintentionally, lost its early commitment to the notion that learning and service must not only be joined so that students can experience communities, learn about and from them, and perhaps leave some lasting impact? The learning and service must be so mutually interdependent that each transforms the other (Honnet & Poulsen, 1989); that one learns about development by doing development.

It can be argued that the source of the wisdom in service learning is in the community. Not only was this field founded in a community setting but the wisdom stories in this book illustrate that the "chance" or the "happenstance" events, as Shumer calls them, (See Chapter 15) overwhelmingly took place in community settings. Perhaps this is because most service-learning pioneers came from or originated their work in community settings. Those who arose in university or school settings were usually not in traditional faculty or staff roles.

This observation may be analogous to a comparison that one of us (Giles) likes to cite. When Willie Sutton, the famous bank robber, was asked why he robbed banks, he replied, "That is where the money is." The wisdom stories here answer the title question of the book, "the community is where the wisdom is."

In the Foreword to the first service-learning history book (Stanton, Giles, & Cruz, 1999) Goodwin Liu (Liu, 1999, p. xii) asked, "What does it mean to enlist the community as a true partner in education?" How we answer that question over the next 50 years will determine what the wisdom for sustaining this movement has been and perhaps can be as we move forward. As readers make their way through this impressive volume, we suggest the following as some questions worthy of reflection.

- How do we construe our work in such a way that it continues to build a safe, secure, and embedded home within higher education institutions while also honoring the wisdom, knowledge, capacities and learning desires of our community partners? Bob Sigmon (1979) asserted that "all the partners in service learning are learners" (p.11). If so, what can we and our students learn from community partners? What may they learn while working with us?

- How do we establish deep, long lasting partnerships with communities and their organizations through which the partners become more than placements for our students? What is our program's and/or our institution's community development agenda (do we have one?) and how do our partnerships fit within and serve these community development goals?

- How might we redefine what distinguishes service learning and relocate it within the larger umbrella of community/civic engagement/scholarship, with a much stronger emphasis, role, and perspective from the community side? Would it include Sigmon's (1979, p. 10) admonition that students' "learning objectives are formed in the context of what needs to be done to serve others?" Would such conceptualization include a greater emphasis on "learning service" (Boyle-Baise et al., 2006) as well as providing it?

There are also questions that beg attention on the institutional, academic side of service learning. Among them might be:

- As practitioners and scholars how do we not lose the critical "eye" and edge we once had when we labored on the margins of higher education or in schools as we continue the effort to institutionalize our work and strengthen the field? How has successful institutionalization of service learning possibly impeded us from reaching our goals for both students and communities?

- Have we adequately understood and outlined just what effective service-learning pedagogy is? For example, can we go beyond talking about the importance of reflection to more specifically and concretely defining and describing what facilitating reflection effectively in the context of specific goals students bring to it—knowledge development; skill building; attitude exploration, etc.—looks like?

- Why do we have such trouble with our field's language whether it be "service-leaning" or "community/civic engagement? What is it about service learning that is so hard to define in a simple, clear way? What do we mean by "learning" in service-learning or civic/community engagement? What do we mean by "service?" What does "engagement" actually mean?

- How and why does service learning appear to develop with different distinguishing features and emphases in different parts of the world? What can we learn, what wisdom can be derived, from comparing and contrasting these efforts and promoting more dialogue among practitioners and scholars across international borders?

- How can we narrow the gap that exists between the goals and outcomes of service-learning research and the learning needs of practitioners and community partners? Might the next 50-year "wisdom" volume include storytelling and wisdom from community partners?

Neither one of us will be around 50 years from now. But if we were to be around, we would be eager to see what has transpired, how this field may have matured and developed. We owe much gratitude to Rob Shumer and his contributors for providing us the opportunity to sit back and ponder these and other questions.

—Dwight E. Giles, Jr.
Timothy K. Stanton

REFERENCES

Boyle-Baise, M., Brown, R., Hsu, M-C., Jones, D., Prakash, A., Rausch, M. et al. (2006). Learning service or service learning: Enabling the civic. *International Journal of Teaching and Learning in Higher Education, 18*(1), 17–26.

Honnet, E. P., & Poulsen. (1989). Principles of good practice in combining service and learning. *A Wingspread special report.* Racine, WI: The Johnson Foundation.

Liu, G. (1999). Foreword. In T. Stanton, D. E. Giles, Jr., & N. Cruz (Eds.), *Service-learning: A movement's pioneers reflect on its origins, practice, and future* (pp. x–xiv). San Francisco, CA: Jossey-Bass.

Sigmon, R. (1979). Service-learning: Three principles. National Center for Service-Learning, ACTION. *Synergist, 8*(1), 9–11.

Sigmon, R. L. (1995). *An organizational journey to service-learning,* Washington, DC: Council of Independent Colleges.

Stanton, T., Giles, D. E., Jr., & Cruz, N., (1999) *Service-learning: A movement's pioneers reflect on its origins, practice, and future.* San Francisco, CA: Jossey-Bass.

WISDOM

The Ultimate Goal of Education and Learning

Wisdom is defined in many ways. It is referred to as accumulated knowledge or erudition or enlightenment. It also is described as "the trait of utilizing knowledge and experience with common sense and insight; the ability to apply knowledge or experience or understanding or common sense and insight." It appears from these definitions that key concepts of the term include applying knowledge or using knowledge and experience. Thus, wisdom goes beyond knowing something; it includes the notion of using knowledge and experience in ways that make common or reasonable sense.

Robert Sternberg, director of the Center for Psychology of Abilities, Competencies, and Expertise at Yale University, has suggested we need to teach for wisdom, not knowledge (Sternberg, 2003). He suggests that intelligence is composed of three constructs: analytical knowledge and skills, creative knowledge and skills, and practical knowledge/skills. Thus, developing wise students requires the cultivation of all three concepts of knowledge and skill in areas related to analyzing knowledge and information, developing creative interpretations and applications of those analyses, and conceiving of that knowledge and information in terms of practical applications. It always results in using knowledge to demonstrate reasonable approaches to doing things.

It appears from these concepts that wisdom is dependent on practical experience, which informs a knowledge base, is tempered with some creative

Where's the Wisdom in Service-Learning?, pages xv–xvi
Copyright © 2017 by Information Age Publishing
All rights of reproduction in any form reserved.

observations/understandings, and manifests itself through application in new settings. Wisdom is thus dependent on age...the assumption that the older you are, the more experience you have, and the more opportunity you have to engage experiences with practical outcomes. Wisdom doesn't necessarily come with age, but it certainly can contribute the additional opportunities to observe knowledge applied in the real world.

It is one goal of this book to demonstrate the wisdom of a few people who have been involved in the service-learning movement for more than the last 30+ years. They have seen the ups and downs of service-learning over this time period and hopefully can share with us important notions about what they have learned from these experiences and what younger people can do in the future to ensure the sustainability of the practice and continue to show that it has made a difference in schools and society.

BIBLIOGRAPHY

Sternberg, R. J. (2003, November). What is an "expert student?" *Educational Researcher, 32*(8), 5–9.

ACKNOWLEDGMENTS

I would like to thank the people from the International Association for Research on Service Learning and Community Engagement and the National Society for Experiential Education who recommended names of individuals who might contribute to the book. Several suggested that we draw from a broader list who served in the K–12 world, as well as the community-based efforts in the country.

I would especially like to thank Dwight Giles and Tim Stanton who agreed to write the introduction/preface and who helped to suggest some of the contributors. Their history with a previous book dealing with the "pioneers" helped to expand the foundation of the effort and to ensure that the book added additional information and perspectives not found in their earlier work.

I would also like to thank my family, especially my wife, Susan, for encouraging me to pursue this effort and who provided insights into how the book could be worthwhile. She provided an additional dose of wisdom to the stories, plus a little editing, as well.

Where's the Wisdom in Service-Learning?, page xvii
Copyright © 2017 by Information Age Publishing
All rights of reproduction in any form reserved.

CHAPTER 1

HISTORY AND PRECURSORS OF SERVICE-LEARNING THEORY, DEVELOPMENT, AND RESEARCH

Robert Shumer, Timothy K. Stanton, and Dwight E. Giles, Jr.

The history of service learning is rooted in three concepts: the common good, civil society, and learning by doing. Each plays a major role in laying the foundation for the ideas contained in the term. As these constructs have evolved and developed over time, they provide a framework to understand service learning in today's world.

What is the common good? In *Common Fire: Leading Lives of Commitment in a Complex World* (Parks Daloz, Keen, Keen, & Daloz Parks, 1996), the authors struggle with an understanding of something they call "the commons."

Many Americans in an earlier time, and some even today, participate in some kind of a commons—a shared, public space of the sort that anchored the American vision of democracy. One form was the classic New England green ringed by the town hall, grange, courthouse, general store, post office,

Where's the Wisdom in Service-Learning?, pages 1–32
Copyright © 2017 by Information Age Publishing
All rights of reproduction in any form reserved.

church, and a flock of households. Other forms of the commons were the square at the county seat in the South, the bodega in the Latino community, Main Street in Middle America, a ballpark, school, temple or cathedral in the city, or the fishing wharf on the coast.

Whatever its form, the commons marked the center of a shared world. Despite sometimes sharp difference, the good of the commons—the good of all—could be worked at, figured out and figured out again...people met and talked together with some sense of shared stake, something in common...the commons is a place where the diverse parts of a community come together and hold a conversation within a shared sense of participation and responsibility. (p. 2)

The commons was a place where people shared a joint interest they all understood, that required participation and a sense of responsibility. In early societies the common good was not abstract, but rather a shared role in society understood by all. Life was relatively simple.

As society became more complicated with larger social groups and more division of labor, understanding of the commons became more abstract. People did not interact with one another every day and jobs became more specialized. With this specialization the notion of shared public space, shared understanding, and shared purpose became more amorphous. What was deemed good for one was not necessarily good for all. This specialization and distancing became more pronounced as social groups began to separate by power and wealth. Kings, nobility, and the wealthy had different roles and functions in society compared to those without money or power. Society began to drift into separate camps where what was common became less clearly understood.

As people began to separate by station, status, and place, the concept of civil society came into being. Owing its birth to the Scottish Enlightenment, Adam Ferguson (1995) suggested civil society "represented the realm of civilization and rising standards of living based on specialization, or the division of labor" (Edwards, Foley, & Diani, 2001, p. 2). As interests became more diverse, people were less willing to unite for common purposes. In this process, citizenship became less socially contextualized. Hegel (1945) also tried to reconcile the division of labor with the ideal of the common citizen. "Civil society is juxtaposed with the state" (p. 2), determining whether the state or other entities would provide the services needed by society. For Italian philosopher Antonio Gramsci (1971), the "heart of civil society provides the arena in which subordinate classes may contest the dominance of the ruling class crystallized in the state" (p. 2). Ultimately, the ideals of a civil society evolve into a tension between who provides the services necessary to alleviate the differences between class and station and who is responsible for programs to meet the needs of the society. This tension permeates every level of social service systems, posing questions about whether public, private, or both deliver services to society.

Add the notion of democracy to these concepts of common good and civil society and we begin to complete the foundational pillars of service learning. As we explore Tocqueville's (1835/1968) concepts of democracy and voluntary associations studied in America in the 19th century, we learn that democracy is not only a form of government, it is a social condition (p. 22). Tocqueville suggests that democracy can work even if the state does not. This means that through voluntary associations in societies such as the United States, informal groups actually compete with the state for the loyalty of citizens (p. 24).

In fact, voluntary organizations can challenge the effectiveness of government. Perhaps a good example is the role of the American Red Cross in delivering disaster relief. While it is a community-based organization, it competes with government structures to ensure that citizens are taken care of during natural and man-made disasters. Citizens might rely more on the Red Cross than they do on the Federal Emergency Management Agency (FEMA), setting up a tension between private and public associations responsible for serving the common good in times of disaster.

As democracy functions both as a governmental organization and a social condition, it sets up a requirement for individuals, notably youth, to learn how the social system functions. Enter into this discussion the philosophy of John Dewey, American pragmatist who describes the relationship between learning about democracy and learning, in general. In his most concise statement on education, *Experience and Education* (Dewey, 1938), he describes the fundamental role experience plays in the learning process and the role schools should play in society. He bemoans the separation of traditional schools from society, suggesting that education must be about life as it is lived and be intimately connected to the social processes of a society. He says "all genuine education comes from experience, but that does not mean that all experiences are genuinely or equally educative" (Dewey, 1938, p. 25). To be educative, experience must demonstrate the criteria of continuity and interaction.

Such experience must be built on a continuum of actions, where reflection on one experience helps to better understand subsequent ones. As this process occurs, there is an interaction between the external and the internal, between what is going on outside the person and what is going on inside, in their emotion and in their psyche. Experience is digested or understood through reflection, a process that suspends action and allows the individual to integrate the experienced situation into his/her knowledge and skill base. Dewey saw this continuous interchange as part of the scientific method, where one uses experience, observation, and analysis to move from one educational plane to another. As long as this movement is positive, growth is occurring.

In connecting schools to society, learning must be rooted in experience and manifest itself in doing, or action. For Dewey, living in a democratic society requires learning about democracy by participating and interacting in ways that continuously grow the individual's ability to function as a citizen. As education is joined with the outside world, students become exposed to curriculum that is relevant and necessary for understanding the foundational principles of social interaction. This means that curriculum must be student-centered, where learning topics come from the real world settings in which students are engaged and then enhanced in the classroom. By applying the scientific method of observing, hypothesizing, and analyzing ideas and activities, one continuously seeks to broaden his/her command of theories and concepts, the transportable knowledge that prepares one for the next learning adventure.

Lastly, Dewey believes learning begins with an impulse, an intrinsic desire to know, and manifests itself through a purpose, or a reason to know and understand. Developing a purpose requires the formulation of a plan or an agenda for acquiring and utilizing knowledge. Ultimately, to allow for growth and control, all knowledge must be applied.

In *Experience and Education* Dewey states that the ultimate purpose of education is self-control. This concept of self-control is very important to citizens in a democracy. Dewey echoes Tocqueville's words when he says: "democracy is more than a form of government, it is primarily a mode of associated living, of conjoint communicated experience" (Dewey, 1916, p. 87). The goal of education in a democracy is to expose young people to society through inquiry in order to develop self-thinking ability. This is a social role only fulfilled by schools. Since, as Socrates noted, a slave is "one who accepts from another the purposes which control his conduct" (Dewey, 1916, p. 85), the goal of education is to allow youth to develop independence and not rely on others to control their behavior.

These ideas are further discussed in a major publication on the theory of experiential learning (Warren, Sakofs, & Hunt, 1995). In a collection of articles on these topics the authors discuss the historical, philosophical, social, and psychological foundations of experiential education. In one article, Joplin (1995) discusses the essential elements of experiential education programs. They include: (a) student-based rather than teacher based, (b) personal not impersonal nature, (c) process and product orientation, (d) evaluation for internal and external reasons, (e) holistic understanding and component analysis, (f) organized around experience, (g) perception based rather than theory based, and (h) individual based rather than group based. Thus, experiential learning is a process based approach to learning that focuses on individual experiences, and emphasizes the impact of experience on the life of the learner.

Csikzentmihalyi (Csikzentmihalyi, M. & Csikzentmihalyi, I., 1988; & Csikzentmihalyi, 1990) captures all these elements of experiential learning at the end of the 20th century. In what he describes as "flow," a condition of the optimal experience, action, feedback, loss of self, loss of time, total engagement, and intrinsic motivation are all critical elements. These factors combine to produce autotelic learners, driven by the joy of the learning experience itself.

Dewey, Csikzentmihalyi, and others describe a process of learning by doing that generically outlines the activities embedded in service learning. Service learning is a special form of experiential learning, where the learning experiences always revolve around the service activities. Learners reflect on their service to make meaning of the process and to ensure that everyone involved is engaged in learning by doing.

Origins of the Modern Service-Learning Movement

Using these three foundational pillars—the common good, civil society, and learning by doing, we begin to understand the formulation and development of the service-learning movement over the last 40 years. A term coined by Bob Sigmon and Bill Ramsay at the Oak Ridge Lab in 1967, service learning was defined as "the accomplishment of tasks that meet genuine human needs in combination with conscious educational growth (Stanton, Giles, & Cruz, 1999, p. 2). Many other definitions have been offered. Stanton, in *Service-Learning: Groping Toward a Definition* (Stanton, 1990), claims service-learning is "more of a program emphasis than a type of program, representing educational, social, and political values" (p. 67). It is a philosophy of performing service to others in order to bring about social justice and empower those without power. He suggests Sigmon's (1979) three principles of service learning help define the relationship between servers and those served: (a) those being served control the services provided, (b) those being served become better able to serve and be served by their own actions, and (c) those who serve are also learners and have significant control over what is expected to be learned. There is an empowering element to service, not just helping for the sake of helping. "There is a social exchange between the service-learner and those being served." Thus, service learning is either a form of experiential learning, or it is a philosophy of experiential education which "suggests methods and practices that should inform all programs" (p. 67). Perhaps, he says, "it is both."

A Delphi study (Shumer 1993) reinforced the notion that service learning was a complex term. Service learning could only be understood in terms of the context of the experiences had by the participants. Identifying 11 school-based models and 15 community based examples, (along with 25 "continua") the study suggested that service learning is only understood when you know the purpose, the goals, the activities, and the impacts. There are many dimensions to each program. This complexity is revealed in the conclusion, where the authors suggest "service learning is an amorphous concept that resists rigid definitions and universal understanding." These definitions and principles suggest that service learning is broad and complex in its meaning and description.

Some also believe that the notion of reciprocity (see Stanton, 1990b) separates service learning from volunteerism, community service, and experiential education. There is an expectation that those providing the service will learn from those being served. Service learning is not just charitable giving, or a one-way process where a person or group provides service and the others only receive goods and services (Kahne & Westheimer, 1996). Rather, those who serve learn something about the causes and conditions of those in need of service, and hopefully, through the experience can more adequately influence society to enact more long lasting, satisfying solutions to society's problems.

In a book about pioneers of the service-learning movement (Stanton, Giles, & Cruz, 1999), Seth Pollack develops a chart explaining reasons why people came to the service-learning movement (p. 20). The motivation of the pioneers was to provide one of three things: service or charity, social justice, or democratic education. As Stanton, Giles, & Cruz also demonstrate, there were 27 precursors or strands of service learning including the term itself (Appendix A, 1999). One of the motivating forces for many programs and early pioneers was the religious activism of the 1950s and 1960s that was manifested in the Civil Rights Movement and the religious opposition to the Vietnam War. One of the programmatic manifestations of service learning came through office of campus ministry, such as at Vanderbilt University where the chaplain, who had led civil rights efforts, later developed opportunities for students to serve in ways that addressed issues of social justice. It is also interesting to note that at least seven of the pioneers, most of who are detailed in the history of the movement, had graduated from theological seminaries and demonstrated commitments to service and social justice. It is interesting, if not instructive to note that four of the pioneers, John Duley, Robert Sigmon, Garry Hesser, and Dwight Giles had graduated from Union Theological Seminary in New York across the span of three decades; this is probably not an accidental connection given Union's longstanding commitment to social action and social justice. Thus, one of the bases of motivation for the movement was a cluster of "spiritual seeds." (Stanton, Giles, & Cruz, 1999, pp. 49–52.) The questions they addressed included: (a) How does education serve society?; (b) What is the relationship between service and social change?; and (c) What is the purpose of education in a democracy? These three constructs actually restate service learning's foundational roots. In different words, they ask: (a) What is the common good and how is it served?; (b) How are inequities dealt with in a civil society and who is responsible for addressing those issues?; and (3) What needs to be taught in schools that exist in democratic societies so that students learn how to function as citizens and maintain democratic processes?

Frameworks Are Added to Concepts

Fundamentally, these important concepts drive the service-learning movement. Yet, in the last several decades of the 20th century, from the time the term originated, service-learning ideals have been carried through a variety of other frameworks or programs. Although not necessarily called service learning, these initiatives have embraced the ideas and ideals of service learning and moved them in new directions, actually incubating them in different homes, carrying them to new iterations in each decade. There is a pattern of people, institutions, and organizations that created networks and pathways to move service learning forward. There were at least four distinctive periods of development: origin/incubation, taking root, growth, and moving toward mainstream. This chapter will trace the movement through the four periods in both K–12 and Higher Education arenas, noting that things seem to grow and develop during the 80s and 90s, and to begin to fragment again in the new century.

1970S: A PERIOD OF INCUBATION AND NURTURING

K–12 Education

In the K–12 arena, the career education/vocational education movement contributed greatly to the development of service-learning principles and provided a host of people and institutions that have been involved in the proliferation of service learning to the present time. Career and vocational programs focused on the concept of learning by doing and were grounded in Dewey's philosophy of education.

Experience-Based Career Education (EBCE) was one of the largest federal initiatives in the 1970s. Started as an effort to better connect students with employers and community agencies for purposes of career exploration and career knowledge, four regional educational laboratories developed model programs and then expanded those models to schools across the country. The Far West Lab (San Francisco, CA) and Northwest Labs

(Portland, OR) were two that developed comprehensive models of EBCE, based on Dewey's principles of experiential learning. They conducted research that showed students grew in career knowledge and maintained parity with traditional students in academic subjects (Spotts & Evenson, 1977; Owens, 1982). More than 100 studies were conducted on EBCE that showed it was educationally sound (Anderson & Drucker, 1976; Bucknam & Brand, 1983). Other studies (Smith & Theophano, 1976) showed that the use of reflection, highly touted in the design, was not utilized effectively and was actually missing in many settings.

Experience-Based Career Education, along with other career programs, helped to develop research connections between universities in the vocational education network: UC Berkeley, University of Minnesota, Ohio State University, UCLA, and Brandeis University. Personal connections were made and relationships developed between individuals at the universities and educational labs. As a result, a network was established that would provide support to the service-learning movement throughout the rest of the century. For example, the Northwest Lab continues to this day to be a lead partner for the Corporation for National and Community Service in national service literacy programs and was a partner in the National Service-Learning Clearinghouse throughout the 1990s. The University of Minnesota developed the first National Service-Learning Clearinghouse, of which UCLA later became the higher education center. UCLA, along with its Higher Education Research Institute, began to include questions about service in their national research on university freshmen, and have contributed enormously to the field. UC Berkeley houses the National Service Learning Research and Development Center. The University of Minnesota has been the lead research institution on career and technical education, housing the National Center for Research on Career and Technical Education. Some of its partners continue to be the Ohio State University, UC Berkeley, and the Northwest Lab.

Other initiatives were developing in the 1970s that promoted community-based, experiential learning at the K–12 level. In the late 1960s the National Commission on Resources for Youth (NCRY, n.d., 1975) embarked on a national effort to expand opportunities for young people to assume active, responsible roles in their communities. Established by a retired juvenile court judge, Mary Conway Kohler, NCRY set out to draw attention to the lack of youth participation in communities, carry out studies of community organizations and schools attempting to carve out new responsible roles for youth, and catalyze networking and dialogue among practitioners and other experts in order to propel youth participation to national prominence. Many NCRY associates became service learning's early pioneers, whether as researchers (Dan Conrad, Diane Hedin), or practitioners (Gib Robinson, Joan Schine, Tim Stanton).

The Mott Foundation in Michigan supported the development of a Community Schools network. Such programs expanded educational opportunities to the entire community by utilizing school facilities as places where parents, youth, and community members could go after school hours to enjoy the opportunity to continue learning. Community Schools nurtured the concepts of the "commons," believing that bringing people together through the schools would help build a sense of community and expand opportunities for everyone to participate in life-long learning.

Philanthropic/Foundation Support

The Mott Foundation involvement exemplifies a number of foundations and organizations that often provided initial and primary philanthropic support to the community and service-learning movement. Mott supported the notions of common good, experiential learning and civil society of service learning, believing that schools could function as effective centers of learning and social integration. Mott originally funded the Community Schools movement in the 1960s, supporting the use of school facilities as community centers to provide programming for youth and adults during after-school hours. While not yet described as service learning, community schools worked to physically connect schools with community groups and organizations to facilitate learning, recreation, and meet the educational, cultural, and development needs of a community. Mott went on to fund a variety of initiatives, all based on the foundational principles of service learning, including: after-school programming and several initiatives in service learning, helping to train and develop service-learning practitioners and model school-community connections.

A host of foundations which believed in the three pillars of service learning followed Mott's example. This input from philanthropic groups also supported the ideals of service and community assistance. Foundations such as Ford (support for community work and civic engagement), Kettering (civil society and civic engagement), Kaufman (community involvement and community development), Kellogg (community development, youth development, and later service learning itself), Surdna (civic engagement and citizenship education, Lilly (development of volunteerism and civic participation), DeWitt-Wallace (community service and civic engagement), the Johnson Foundation (national meetings on service-learning, character education, and civic engagement), State Farm (service learning, civic engagement). These philanthropic agencies sought to develop university/school/community-based programs that addressed learning by doing and contributed something for the good of society and individual citizens.

Higher Education

The 1970s also saw the origins of service learning in colleges and universities. Early practitioners in these programs founded two national organizations to support their work, the Society for Field Experience Education and the National Center for Public Service Internships in 1971. The Society for Field Experience Education focused on field-based learning (Dewey's principles) and the National Center for Public Service Internships emphasized public (mostly government) service (civil society). Both developed a following and eventually merged in 1978 into the National Society for Internships and Experiential Education (NSIEE). As its name states, the focus of NSIEE was on the development and promotion of experiential education through field study, internships, community-based courses (some now called service learning), which engaged university students in service projects, focused on issues of civil society, attempting to address social problems. NSIEE became one of the more innovative organizations in higher education for the next two decades, promoting programs, research, and advocacy for experiential and service-learning programs for both high school and higher education.

Another initiative in the 1970s promoted community service projects in higher education. The University Year for ACTION, supported by federal funds, engaged more than 10,000 college students from 100 colleges and universities (Kendall & Associates, 1990) in service programs throughout the country. The University Year for ACTION helped fuel the fires of service and create a network of people and institutions that were devoted to promoting principles of service and service learning through attention to issues of the civil society.

By the end of the decade, the National Student Volunteer Program changed its name to the National Center for Service-Learning, reflecting its intention to support and institutionalize service learning across secondary and postsecondary education. The National Center for Service-Learning produced a journal, *Synergist*, which distributed many articles of research and practice about service learning. Almost everyone who would contribute to service learning's "taking root" movement in the 1980s published something in *Synergist* before its demise, along with the National Center, in the early 1980s.

Conclusions

Clearly the origins of service learning, focusing on the principles of the common good, civil society and experiential education, were well established in the 1970s. Numerous K–12 schools and institutions of higher education developed programs that promoted foundational principles. Add to these accomplishments new and renewed initiatives in community-based organizations, such as the YMCA and University Extension, along with organizations in adult education, such as the Council for Adult and Experiential Education (CAEL), which promoted early concepts of assessing and accrediting prior, experienced-based learning, and you find a broad movement of ideas ready to take root.

The Decade of the 1980s—Service Learning Takes Root

The 1980s saw service-learning organizations begin to work together. Literature began to appear like never before, and the intellectual and practical forces fought to become implanted in their respective homes. Most important, specific organizations, such as the Campus Compact, which were created to boost young people's engagement in civil society, soon embraced the intellectual principles of service learning and focused on expanding it across post-secondary education.

K–12 Education

The 1980s saw service learning take root in high schools. In one of the few studies of the prevalence of community service and service attached to the curriculum, it was disclosed that about one-third of the high schools in the country had community service programs, while only about 10% had programs that connected the service with the curriculum (Newmann & Rutter, 1983). This was an important report because it provided a benchmark by which to measure the growth of the movement across time.

CAEL, NSIEE, and the Association for Experiential Education (AEE) issued a joint statement about the importance of experiential learning in education. The joint communiqué was written in response to the national report, *A Nation At Risk*, which sought to bring more traditional forms of classroom based instruction into prominence in K–12 schools. AEE, then headed by its president James Kielsmeier, was an organization of people involved primarily in outdoor education and recreation/active learning programs. AEE brought with it an established journal, the *Journal of Experiential Education*, which became an outlet for more publications on programs, research, and issues of importance to the entire experiential education community. It also had a cadre of practitioners and researchers who were interested in furthering the cause of experiential learning across the board, from educational institution-based, to community-based, to youth organization based settings. AEE helped expand the number of roots taking hold by engaging a new sector, the youth development community, in the service-learning, experiential learning movement.

The youth development connections brought many allies (Hamilton, 1980; NCRY, n.d., 1975; Schine, 1981). The Center for Youth Development Research at the University of Minnesota began focusing on service as one of its areas of interest. Seminal studies by Diane Hedin and Dan Conrad (1982) began to look at service and experiential learning as a vehicle for measuring student learning, social development, and social responsibility. Other youth development educators and researchers, such as Stephen Hamilton at Cornell, connected their research about university extension and 4-H with elements of service and social change. Hamilton (Hamilton, 1981; Hamilton & Frenzel, 1987) was one of the key researchers on youth, studying academic achievement, civic education, apprenticeship, and other related fields.

The 1980s also saw closer connections between and interaction among service-learning advocates in K–12 and postsecondary education. For example, in the early 1980s EBCE joined NSIEE, which, up until then, had been primarily a higher education organization. Rob Shumer, president of the National Experience Based Career Education Association brought a declining organization, along with the Executive High School Internship Program (another career education program), into NSIEE. This was one of the first efforts to connect higher education and K–12 under one umbrella and join people in both sectors that believed in Dewey's principles of experiential learning.

Higher Education

New service-learning programs took root across the spectrum of higher education, including community colleges. Consortia such as the Great Lakes Colleges Association and Higher Education Consortium for Urban Affairs developed and sponsored both domestic and international service-learning programs. Programs birthed in the 1970s, such as field study programs at Cornell University and UCLA, USC's Joint Education Project, and the University Year for Action all matured, setting practice standards for the field. An experienced practitioner group articulated and agreed upon "principles of good practice," which became one of the most sought after publications of The Johnson Foundation[1] (Honnet & Poulsen, 1989). Although the newly elected Reagan Administration closed down the National Center for Service-Learning in 1983, which had encouraged and documented service learning's earliest expressions, NSEE filled its place with service learning increasingly becoming the focus of its conferences and publications.

The Context of Change in Higher Education

However, in spite of these considerable advances, service-learning programs remained few and far between. In the traditional academy, pedagogy was largely unchanged and remained within the realm of academic departments. Concerns with students' moral development and community participation were lodged with student affairs or residence staff, religious groups, or other nonacademic administrators. Service learning remained marginal, but not invisible at most colleges and universities.

However, by the decade's midpoint, two reform movements, one within postsecondary education, and one largely outside, would set the stage for major expansion in service-learning practice and research (Gardener, 1984). Within higher education, there emerged a call for major reform, which questioned both the content and passive, didactic process of postsecondary teaching and learning. The other movement was the response of individuals outside the academy to reports of students' increasingly self-centered attitudes and their efforts to reinvigorate higher education's obligation to challenge students to lead more socially responsible lives. These separate, but parallel, initiatives set the stage for educators who advocated the integration of student service involvement with strategies that promote active learning and critical thinking—the pedagogy of service learning.

Curriculum Reform

American higher education in the 1980s experienced intense self-examination, external criticism, and debate regarding basic goals and purposes. A series of national reports questioned whether curricula met their defined objectives and suggested a fundamental reevaluation of the structure and pedagogy of undergraduate education.[2]

Out of this ferment arose renewed attention to "excellence" in the teaching/learning process and a new focus on the importance of active, experience-based learning. The National Institute of Education's (1984) Study Group on the Conditions of Excellence in American Higher Education recommended that faculty increase their use of "internships and other forms of carefully monitored experiential learning" (p. 27). Kaston and Heffernan (1984), in a study undertaken for the National Endowment for the Humanities, indicated widespread acceptance by faculty of internships and field studies as integral parts of liberal arts education. NSIEE reported growing numbers of requests for assistance from institutions interested in linking classroom instruction to supervised field experience in the community.[3] With greater acceptance and utilization of internships, field studies, and other forms of off-campus learning within higher education, the issue for advocates of experiential education became not so much whether faculty would utilize these methods, but rather how they would use them, both inside and outside the classroom, and how they could effectively assess the learning their students achieved (Kendall, Duley, Little, Permaul, & Rubin, 1986).

This debate on pedagogy and the role of experience began to affect the core liberal arts, as well as applied, practical disciplines. In debates about which content areas should comprise "common learning," or general education, of liberal arts students, educators began to shift their focus from knowledge acquisition to cognitive skill development—"abilities that last a lifetime" (Edgerton, 1984). Research into the undergraduate experience reinforced this thrust, stressing the importance of cognitive skills and the ability to apply one's learning, as benchmarks for student assessment (Loacker, Cromwell, & O'Brien, 1986). The national education reports criticized the passive, impersonal nature of instructional methodologies and called for a pedagogy that was more active and involving, that enabled learners to take more responsibility for their education, and that brought them into direct contact with the subjects of their study. Instructional research demonstrated, the reports said, that learning activities which require learners to apply knowledge and skills to the solution of problems more often develop the higher cognitive skills than do traditional classroom methods (Cross, 1987). The National Institute of Education's (1984) Study Group recommended use of internships and other forms of monitored experiential learning to enable students to become creators, as well as receivers, of knowledge. The learning students obtained from such experiential education opportunities was increasingly seen as linking and integrating their intellectual growth with their moral, personal, and career development.

The Initiative for Public Service

During this same period individuals outside the academy began to question whether higher education was adequately preparing students to live in a society that faced complex and seemingly intractable problems (Boyer, 1987). Echoing the work of NCRY in the 1970s these people worried about research reports that showed students as increasingly isolated and holding narrow, self-centered attitudes.[4]

Advocates of stronger civic participation by students acknowledged that the shift in student attitudes might have been due in part to their perception of more limited economic opportunities. As a response to this situation, educational institutions needed to focus on graduating a citizenry with: a broad understanding of the interdependencies of peoples, social institutions, and communities; an enhanced ability both to draw upon and further develop this knowledge as they confront and solve human problems (Newman, 1985); and a strong commitment to act out ethically and thoughtfully the democratic compact.

In *Higher Education and the American Resurgence* (1985) Education Commission of the States President Newman identified a failure in the structure and content of our educational system. Structurally we had not provided a means of linking classroom study with students' direct experience of social problems and issues. In content areas we had failed to effectively educate students with both an understanding of these social problems and an awareness of the traditional responsibilities of democratic citizenship.

In response college presidents, education scholars, politicians, students and others began to call for integration of the ethic and practice of social involvement, critique and analysis into the mission and values of higher education.[5] The presidents of Brown, Georgetown, and Stanford universities joined Newman to found Campus Compact, a consortium of college and university presidents committed to increasing the level of public service activity among students. In so doing they sought to renew and reinvigorate the public service mission of higher education (Jencks & Riesman, 1968, Waring, 1988).

Soon universities and colleges began to establish public service centers and other structures to enable students to become involved as volunteers, both to provide community service and to develop awareness of public issues and community needs, leadership skills, and a lifelong commitment to social responsibility.

Mutual Concerns, Mutual Benefits

Although these movements—for education reform and for public service—shared a common concern with the basic aims of higher education, they engaged in little sustained, cross-group dialogue. Neither group seriously considered the explicit relationship between public service and the core, *academic* missions of higher education institutions. In the early days of both movements only a few lonely voices addressed the place of community service and what students learn from it within the academic curriculum (Couto, 1982; Luce, et al., 1988; Stanton 1988).

As the public service initiative matured, however, it began to include the goals and values of service learning within its agenda. The existing separation of service from learning was viewed as reflecting higher education's traditional distinction between theory and practice and between teaching and research (Wagner, 1986) and as inhibiting of both the effectiveness of students' service efforts and the depth of their learning while they were involved (Stanton, 1990b).

Campus Compact Project on Integrating Service With Academic Study

Thus, by 1988 Campus Compact executive committee members Donald Kennedy and David Warren had commissioned a study to examine how faculty might play a stronger role in promoting civic responsibility and organized three regional conferences where goals and action steps were discussed.

These conversations led Compact's leadership to launch its "Project on Integrating Service with Academic Study" in 1990. A national advisory board was established composed of individuals who were advocates for linking service with the curriculum, who had stature within the higher education community, and who were in positions to influence change at the national level. A three-year grant was obtained from The Ford Foundation to support implementation of three summer institutes to bring together faculty teams from Campus Compact member institutions for a week-long workshop on combining service with academic study. Historians of this movement view these institutes as perhaps the most pivotal events in service learning's movement from the margins to the mainstream of higher education (Harkavy, 2006).

Research

With practice taking root across K–12 and postsecondary education, and with practitioner networks increasingly connected through NSIEE, CAEL, AEE, Campus Compact and university extension efforts, a dramatic sprouting of another intellectual and conceptual root of service learning took place at this time: service-learning research. Whereas research studies on service and experiential education had been spotty in the 1970s (with most coming from EBCE and other K–12 systems), research in the 1980s focused on all levels of experiential learning, from schools, to communities, to higher education.

Most notably, the associations connected to experiential education, such as NSIEE, began to branch out and establish new roots in organizations which focused on research and evaluation. A research committee was formed in NSEE in the mid-1980s, and that committee connected with the American Educational Research Association (AERA), the largest research organization in the country. A special interest group at AERA on Experiential Education, originally called the Education in Field Settings SIG, was chaired year after year by people who would lead the service-learning field: Dwight Giles, David Moore, Stephen Hamilton, Rob Shumer, Tom Owens, Janet Eyler, and in later decades Andy Furco and Shelley Billig.

Research became even a greater focus for NSIEE. The publication of a *Research Agenda for Experiential Education* (Permaul, Anderson, & Hughes, 1984), called attention to the importance of testing theories of learning through research and publishing research that had value to practitioners.

NSIEE produced its own journal, *Experiential Education,* which contained articles on practice, research, and advocacy.

Conclusions

Up until the mid-1980s service-learning advocates and practitioners were a very small, marginal group within higher education.[6] However, with legitimacy and support conveyed by the "80s" education reform and public service initiatives, interest in service learning began to grow both at secondary and post-secondary levels. What was once a marginal, not well understood form of alternative education was by 1990 suddenly on the front burner of numerous higher education organizations and on the minds of a growing number of campus administrators and faculty.[7] At the K–12 level service-learning practice broadened and strengthened its position in a number of fields: youth development, outdoor education/recreation, university extension and 4-H, adult education, etc. In higher education service learning proliferated across all sectors with NSEE and Campus Compact taking the lead (Duley, 1990). Each new manifestation of the service learning was based, in part, on the foundational themes: common good, civil society, and experiential learning . Such a wide and well rooted idea was ready for further growth and expansion in the next decade.

SERVICE LEARNING'S GROWTH DECADE: THE 1990S

If the 1980s were service learning's "taking root" decade, then the 1990s were surely a growth decade. With its intellectual foundations established and encouragement, advocacy, and professional development opportunities coming from the nation's political leaders and across the spectrum of secondary and postsecondary associations, programs cropped up everywhere, especially following the federal government's establishment of the Corporation for National Service and its Serve America and Learn and Serve America funding programs. By 1991 the U.S. Congress had created the Commission on National and Community Service, which began making grants of $70 million annually to promote volunteer activity across the nation. In 1993, Congress enacted President Clinton's National Service Trust, which formed AmeriCorps and national service opportunities for individuals that would assist them in paying for post-secondary education. Each state was encouraged to form its own service commission to seek and distribute Corporation for National Service (CNS) funds to local school districts, universities, and colleges. Similarly, Campus Compact organized state-level compacts, which also gained financial support from CNS and private foundations, which spawned service learning in their states. By the end of the century most colleges, universities, numerous secondary, and even elementary schools, offered some sort of service-learning program.

K–12 Education

The Corporation for National Service was extremely important to the expansion of service learning, especially at the K–12 level. States were given special allocations of funds, based on the school populations, as well as additional funds to expand and promote service-learning activities. This source of funds, coupled with the efforts at CNS in Washington, D.C. to connect service programs with national organizations, worked as a catalyst to bring many groups and organizations together. CNS worked in the decade to expose many national organizations to service, bringing such groups as the Association for Supervision and Curriculum Development (ASCD), the National Education Association, the American Federation of Teachers, and a host of other professional organizations to integrate service learning into their core values and activities (Schlecty, 1991). For example, ASCD developed a special interest group of more than 200 people in the mid-1990s, producing publications (McPherson & Kinsley, 1995) and training sessions at national and regional conferences. The expansion to other organizations, such as Youth Service America, helped spread the service ideals through youth programs. The Points of Light Foundation, started during the George Herbert Walker Bush era, also collaborated with CNS to expand service programs into the non-profit sector and into community-based organizations. Points of Light sponsored, along with CNS, national conferences that brought people from all kinds of institutions and organizations who work through community organizations to deal with the issues of the civil society.

Higher Education

In addition to its exponential growth during the 1990s, service-learning practice diversified in higher education. For example, at research universities such as Stanford and Duke, practitioners began developing service-learning research programs, enabling students to undertake "public scholarship" in cooperation with and for community-based groups. Other efforts focused on service learning in capstone education (Portland State University), as diversity training (City Year), and increasingly as "civic learning," most strongly exemplified at the new California State University at Monterey Bay, one of the first universities to require service learning of all students. Professional meeting discussions and publications moved from a focus on how to do the work to how to sustain and institutionalize it. Most importantly, both practitioners and researchers, who either developed out of the field or became interested in it, began calling for and carrying out evaluation and research into service learning's outcomes on students, faculty, institutions, and occasionally on the community partners (Giles, Honnet, & Migliore, 1991). They developed models of practice (Essential Elements of Service-Learning, National Service-Learning Cooperative, 1998) as well as models of good practice, assessment and measurement (Alliance for Service-Learning in Educational Reform Principles of Good Practice, 1995, and Shumer's Self Assessment for Service Learning, 2000).

Research practices began to get a boost during this decade. Resources from the Fund for the Improvement of Post Secondary Education (FIPSE) helped produce some of the more important documents in the field. Most notably, FIPSE-funded projects at Vanderbilt University led to the publication of one of the most influential books in the field, *Where's The Learning in Service-Learning* (Eyler & Giles, 1999). This publication was considered by many to be the foundation for evidence that service learning had multiple impacts on everything from academic knowledge and critical thinking to civic awareness and development of inter-personal skills and abilities.

Growth of research funded by FIPSE and other foundations (Kellogg, DeWitt Wallace, Kettering, Pew, & Ford) also lead to the establishment of a formal outlet for articles. *The Michigan Journal for Community Service Learning* was established in 1994 and became the premier publication for professional research on service learning. Over the years special editions, such as the Fall 2000 edition on research, have helped to provide the field with a body of literature that moved service learning from a splintered movement to one with an established research base. Other publications, such as Waterman's *Service Learning: Applications from the Research* (1997) and the American Association for Higher Education's series on *Service Learning in the Disciplines* (Zlotkowski) helped grow the field into a legitimate academic subject of study.

At the K–12 level, Conrad and Hedin's review of the research on service learning (1991) also helped to start a trend for the field. In 2000, Shelley Billig wrote a comprehensive report on service-learning research, with the Conrad and Hedin piece as a model. Skinner and Chapman (1999) would follow the lead of Newmann and Rutter from the 1980s and conduct a study of the prevalence of service learning in American schools. Their study would show that, indeed, service learning had grown from 10% in the 1980s to over 50% in all public high schools, with more than 75% having some form of service activities.

National studies conducted by Brandeis researchers during the 1990s would also help to make the case that service learning had positive impacts on civic outcomes, on academic achievement, and on skills and behaviors (Melchior & Bailis, 2002). Researching CNS programs (Serve America and Learn and Serve), as well as the Active Citizenship Today initiative conducted by The Constitutional Rights Foundation and Close Up Foundation, Melchior and Bailis helped shed light on some of the impacts of service learning on foundational concepts of learning by doing, influencing civil society, and developing a notion of the common good.

Conclusions

What was 20 years before a largely unknown and little navigated pedagogical innovation, was now a maturing field of practitioners and scholars, whose work would soon be a focus of how institutions measure their quality and recruit their students. The groundwork of the 1980s, which fed the growth of the 1990s, moved the field from an assemblage of programs and ideals to a discipline-like field characterized by federal, state, and local policies, supported by research that examined theories and practice, and implemented through a host of professional organizations which supported a professional literature. The 1990s proclaimed that service learning was more than just three loosely coupled foundational ideals and concepts. It was now a vibrant field that was working to establish itself as a legitimate subject with a national and international following.

Educational Reform: Actions That Affected the Service-Learning Movement

While educational reforms were active in the 1970s at the K–12 level through a national focus on career and work-based education, the influence of reform efforts both helped and hindered the service-learning movement in the 1980s and beyond. In each decade reformers called for some the foundational elements of service learning. Experiential learning, connecting with community, and addressing issues of civil society were included in change efforts.

In the 1970s, change initiatives focused on connecting schools with communities for career knowledge. School reform also emphasized values clarification and character education (Glasser, 1965; Leming, 1993), suggesting that youth needed to develop their values, moral, and character compass. These efforts not only pushed schools to consider more than just academic learning, but academic learning that applied to development of the whole student. The service-learning movement grew during this decade, with the formulation and operation of the National Center for Service learning.

Much of the reform effort in the 1980s, 1990s, and into the 21st century followed guidelines established by reform scholars, such as Benjamin Levin. He proposed a theory of four stages of reform: origins, adoption, implementation, and outcomes (Levin, 2001). Each stage was influenced by many interest groups, including teachers and teacher's unions, parents and parent groups, government officials, business interests, and the media. Each group was capable of supporting or derailing any educational reform effort, and in fact, these interest groups clashed throughout each decade, both boosting and undermining the foundational elements of service learning.

As mentioned earlier, several of these reforms were partially derailed by the new report, *A Nation at Risk* (1983), which described American education as failing to prepare youth to compete in the world's economies and complained about the lack of serious academic growth. The report called for renewed emphasis on science and math, and acquisition of the knowledge deemed important to society, such as the Greek classics and formal education. The important part of this reform movement was the de-emphasis of experiential learning (as reflected in the earlier discussed joint communiqué).

While this reform would gather political favor, other reformers were calling for schools which had broader agendas that included some of the foundational principles of service learning. Important books, such as *Horace's Compromise* (Sizer, 1984) and *A Place Called School* (Goodlad, 1984) appeared at the same time criticizing the formality and lack of flexibility of secondary schools. There was renewed focus on dropouts and dropout prevention by engaging youth with the world of work, making schools smaller and more personalized, and connecting youth with community and national service as a means for developing responsibility, civic engagement, career knowledge, and social understanding (William T. Grant Foundation Commission on Work, Family, and Citizenship, 1988; Danzig & Szanton, 1986). An important study by Conrad and Hedin (1982) demonstrated the academic, social, and developmental benefits of community service and experiential learning. The creation of the Coalition of Essential Schools, based on Sizer's work, restarted the movement of model schools that were focused on notions of student-as-worker, mastery learning, teachers as facilitators, and "teaching less so students could learn more." (Sizer, 1992). These reform initiatives moved forward in the 1990s, building on the momentum of the service-learning movement. Service and active, community-based, experiential learning became more closely connected with the Association for Supervision and Curriculum Development (ASCD), which was the largest professional education organization in the country. The special interest group on service learning grew to more than 200 members, and ASCD featured sessions on service learning at its national conferences. By 1995, ASCD had sponsored many work-shops and meetings on service learning. In many ways this development connected service learning with mainstream reform initiatives.

Then, at the K–12 level, service-learning reforms were again set back in 2002, this time by national legislation known as the No Child Left Behind Act. The law, designed to improve elementary and secondary education by introducing accountability back into the system through high stakes test-ing, had a dampening effect on educational programs that connected stu-dents with the community, such as service learning, vocational education, and internships/apprenticeships. As with the 1980s, the focus was again on rigorous classroom-based instruction, especially aimed at basic skills of reading and mathematics.

At the post-secondary level, cyclical reforms on active and passive learn-ing, again, especially community-connected programs such as service learning were restricted by academic attitudes enforcing the "Platoniza-tion of education" (Harkavy, 2004). Such attitudes embraced Plato's elitist view that education should be contemplative and aristocratic, not active and connected to society. Harkavy explains this perspective by citing the work of Stanley Fish, Dean at the University of Illinois (2003), who sug-gests that

> professors cannot possibly provide that kind of learning [preparing under-graduates for lives of civic engagement] and should never try to provide it. Their job is simply to teach what their discipline calls for them to teach and to try to make their students into good disciplinary researchers. Professors cannot make their students into good people . . . and shouldn't try. (p. C5)

Educational reformers' recommendations for more active learning to develop civic knowledge, skills, and dispositions in every decade (for ex-ample, Boyer, 1987), has been thwarted by this mentality. Even though service-learning programs continue to grow in higher education during the 21st century, thinkers such as Fish and his colleagues seek to under-mine its growth and expansion at every turn. This dismissal of the civic and service purposes of community-connected education has contributed to service learning remaining on the margins of higher education. While this battle between advocates of service learning and civic responsibility (Colby, Ehrlich, Beaumont, & Stephens, 2003) and traditional educators continues, the tide seems to be turning toward much greater inclusion of service learning and civically minded programs in all colleges and universities.

THE 21ST CENTURY: 2000–2007

Service Learning Moves Toward Adulthood

Armed with professional organizations, an established literature and research base, and supported by a society that increasingly called for increased service from its citizens, service learning marched into the 21st Century ready to function in adult roles. It would take its place at education and service tables as a peer, a field that had matured over 30 years, ready to continue its quest to be a key part of American education and culture.

K–12 Education

The K–12 community started the new decade by initiating a national organization that spanned all 50 states and engaged individuals from all levels of education: policy makers, teachers, administrators, parents, and like-minded organizations. The National Service-Learning Partnership (NSLP), which got its momentum from the successful National Service-Learning Conference, sponsored by the National Youth Leadership Council, created a network of 8500 people committed to furthering the cause of service learning as a core part of every young person's education. Sponsored by the Academy for Education and Development, the basic theoretical framework of the partnership was that of service-learning was a teaching method that engaged young people in community and school problem solving as part of their academic program (National Service-Learning Partnership, 2006). The NSLP provided a new publication series for the field, *Service-Learning Advances,* which promoted new ideas in practice and updates on federal and state legislative initiatives. Principles of civil society and learning by doing continued to drive the movement's organizations, focusing on learning by doing in the community, connecting academic studies with planned learning programs.

The NSLP added another dimension to the service-learning movement: advocacy. One of the goals of the organization was to provide a presence at the federal level to represent the interests of the service-learning field regarding national legislation affecting programs that promoted service, service learning, and volunteerism. The NSLP would join other national organizations, such as Campus Compact, to advocate for financial support to encourage young people, from elementary school through graduate school, to engage in community-connected learning.

Along with the NSLP, the National Service-Learning Conference would come into its own in the 21st century, bringing more than 2500 individuals together on a yearly basis to discuss all aspects of service. The conference brought stronger international representation and was successful in continuing to engage foundational support (from W. K. Kellogg Foundation and then from State Farm) to help the meetings grow in size and in depth of information sharing.

Other national initiatives characterized the new decade. In 2001, the first International Service-Learning Research Conference, which reconnected K–12 and Higher Education, was held in Berkeley, California. Meetings have been held every year since, and in 2007 the organization became an independent professional association, the International Association for Research on Service-Learning and Community Engagement. The organization brought together researchers from across the country and overseas to discuss service-learning research. A notable outcome for the movement was the development of a book series, *Advances in Service Learning Research.* The publication, edited by Shelley Billig (2002–2007) and guest editors (usually conference sponsors) has produced some of the best research articles of the decade. The book series has also expanded the field to include international contributors, helping to make the movement more of an international phenomenon. The international field expanded when the first international conference on teacher education was held in Brussels in 2007, sponsored by the International Center on Teacher Education at Clemson University.

Civic Missions

The Education Commission of the States, which sponsored the birth of Campus Compact in the 1980s and became involved in tracking state and national legislation related to service learning and civic education in the 1990s, initiated a new program, the Civic Mission of the Schools, in 2002. This project, funded by the Kellogg Foundation, attempts to study ways that young people learn about government and the democratic process by engaging in civic education programs that emphasize simulations, service learning, and other active learning methods of instruction. That initiative, coupled with a parallel program, Project 540, sponsored by the Pew Foundation, sought to engage young people in discussing and solving social problems through active modes of learning, including service learning. Another initiative that started in the 1990s and is continuing to grow as an established approach in the 21st Century, is Public Achievement. Sponsored by the Humphrey Institute on Citizenship and Public Service at the University of Minnesota, this effort recruits college students to work as coaches with middle and high school students to address public issues by learning civic skills necessary to solve community problems. Public Achievement has taken on an international orientation, with programs initiated in Northern Ireland, Israel, Palestine, Turkey, South Africa, and several Balkan States.

Postsecondary Education

This trend in program development is also expressed in higher education as exemplified by Campus Compact. Their focus on service learning in the late 80s and 90s has given way to a much greater emphasis on civic and community engagement. Service and service learning are two components of the overall effort, but they are not the focus, as in earlier decades. Like the Humphrey Institute's emphasis on citizenship and public service, higher education service-learning programs all over the country are including civic engagement and public service in their titles. Perhaps one of the newest models for the 21st century is Tufts University's Jonathan M. Tisch College for Citizenship and Public Service. This university-wide initiative is designed to support the development of college students as active citizens making making the values and skills of citizenship a main part of a Tufts education. The goal is to make sure students graduate ready to be citizens and leaders who are active in building their communities and society. Tisch provides an endowment to fund financial support to students (similar to the Bonner Foundation scholarships) who participate in activities that encourage new ideas that create positive change in communities and engage in groups and organizations that address real community needs.

A second distinguishing feature in service learning's development in this new century has been increasing emphasis on partnerships as the basis for program development and sustainability. Principles of effective community-university partnerships have been articulated and disseminated by Community-Campus Partnerships for Health and other organizations that guide practitioners in their work with community-based organizations for service-learning and community-based research, helping to ensure a strong community voice in program design, development, and evaluation. The partnership concept also stresses long-term engagement between campuses and community groups as a means to help ensure positive and progressive community impact from the work of students and faculty.

Finally, as they did in the mid-1980s with the establishment of Campus Compact, university and college presidents are again providing public leadership to the field, this time in collaboration with civic leaders domestically and overseas. For example, in 2005 Tufts University's President Lawrence Bacow convened 29 university presidents, rectors and vice chancellors from 23 countries in Tailloires, France, "to catalyze and support a worldwide movement of individuals and institutions dedicated to promoting the civic roles and social responsibilities of higher education." The conference participants signed the Talloires Declaration on the Civic Roles and Social Responsibilities of Higher Education, committing to a series of action steps and demonstrating the signatories' commitment to elevating the civic and social mission of their universities (see http://www.tufts.edu/talloiresnetwork/). In similar fashion, presidents and academic leaders from the United States, Europe, and other countries convened a Global Forum sponsored by the Council of Europe's Steering Committee for Higher Education and Research in close cooperation with the International Consortium for Higher Education, Civic Responsibility and Democracy. At the forum, a declaration was adopted by acclamation that affirms the need to increase the commitment of higher education institutions to a democratic culture and sustainable societies and calls for action to promote the principles of democratic citizenship, human rights and civic responsibility in higher education (see http://dc.ecml.at/).

Conclusion

Three concepts, the common good, civil society, and learning by doing, have been the foundational ideas behind the development of service learning over the past 40 years. From alternative schools, to career education, to University Year for Action, to outdoor education, to civic engagement, these three principles have emerged and evolved. From origins of service for charitable purposes, to undoing the inequities of civil society, to a current focus on civic and community engagement, service learning has maintained positive elements of the three ideals. Existing in various levels of adoption, these three concepts have been present, to some degree, in every program or initiative that has helped to deliver community-based learning in its myriad forms. From schools, to colleges and universities, to community settings, people have embraced service learning because they believe it has value for the learner, those served, and the general society that supports the work.

People continue to seek the commons, to understand what makes them part of a community, a state, a nation, and a world. They seek to determine, as we live lives of specialized occupations (often living in isolated or closed communities), how to solve the problems of social injustice, unequal access, unequal opportunity, and varied ownership of resources. They do so by constructing educational systems, both formal and informal, that engage young people in experiences that teach them about their government, their social system and responsibilities, and their ability to survive and thrive in a world filled with challenge and comfort.

As service learning evolves toward a global phenomenon, thriving in Argentina, Canada, Japan, Korea, Ireland, Northern Ireland, Singapore,

South Africa, Australia, and many other nations, the search for the commons will be a constant. Along with concern for civil society and how we continue traditions of democratic rule through experiential learning, service learning will be at the forefront of discussion. Armed with these three foundational principles, it will be a positive force for addressing society's most critical issues.

NOTES

1. Information gained from telephone conversation with Ellen Porter Honnet, spring, 1992.
2. See: Integrity in the College Classroom: A Report to the Academic Community, The Findings and Recommendations of the Project on Redefining the Meaning and Purpose of Baccalaureate Degrees, Association of American Colleges, 1985; Bennett, William J., To Reclaim a Legacy: A Report on the Humanities in Higher Education, National Endowment for the Humanities, 1984; Boyer, Ernest L., College: The Undergraduate Experience In America, Harper & Row for the Carnegie Endowment for the Advancement of Teaching, 1987; Gaff, Jerry G., General Education Today: A Critical Analysis of Controversies, Practices, and Reforms, Jossey-Bass, 1983; Involvement in Learning: Realizing the Potential of American Higher Education, Final Report of the Study Group on the Conditions of Excellence in American Higher Education, National Institute of Education, 1984.

   A thoughtful analysis of the findings in these reports is provided by: Kimball, Bruce A., "The Historical and Cultural Dimensions of the Recent Reports on Undergraduate Education," 1987 Lecture for the Fund for the Improvement of Postsecondary Education delivered to the Lilly Endowment Workshop on the Liberal Arts, June 1987.
3. From NSIEE annual reports, 1985–1991, National Society for Internships and Experiential Education, Raleigh, NC.
4. According to annual ACE-UCLA surveys of freshmen, since 1972 students were attaching decreasing importance to values such as helping others, promoting racial understanding, cleaning up the environment, participation in community action and keeping up with political affairs. During the same period, the percentage of students placing high priority on being well off financially jumped from 40 to 73%. The goal of "developing a meaningful quality of life" showed the greatest decline, almost 50%.

   Surveys by the Carnegie Foundation for The Advancement of Teaching and the Independent Sector indicated similar trends.
5. For example, the American Association for Higher Education in 1986 convened an "action community" of faculty and administrators to examine strategies to increase student involvement in community service. The Council for Liberal Learning of the American Association of Colleges and Universities examined the importance of combining academic study with structured community experiences in the development of student insight into the nature of

public leadership. The Kettering Foundation expanded its series of "Campus Conversations on the Civic Arts," and organized regional faculty seminars and training events. Responding to a directive from their state legislature the California State University and University of California systems prepared plans for implementing a "Human Corps" concept, which strongly encouraged all students to engage in community service. Finally, despite the predominate mood on most campuses, new student leadership emerged through organizations such as the Campus Outreach Opportunity League.

6. Indeed, at annual conferences of the National Society for Internships and Experiential Education (NSIEE) workshops were offered on "working on the margins," or on "life as a marginal professional" for several years.

7. Both Campus Compact and NSIEE reported large increases in inquiries about service learning. The National Youth Leadership Council developed a national service-learning training program. Discipline organizations (e.g., American Sociology Association, American Political Science Association) organized service-learning workshops at their conferences.

REFERENCES

Anderson, S., & Drucker, C. (1976). Experience based career education in Oakland, California: An anthropological perspective. External evaluators' final report on EBCE programs. Volume 3. Berkeley, CA: Educational Testing Service.

Billig, S. et al. (2002–2007). *Advances in service-learning research*. Greenwich, CT: Information Age.

Boyer, E. L., (1987). *College: The undergraduate experience in America*. New York, NY: Harper & Row.

Bucknam, R., & Brand, S. (1983). EBCE really works: A meta-analysis on experience-based career education. *Educational Leadership, 40*(6), 66–71.

Colby, A., Ehrlich, T., Beaumont, E., & Stephens, J. (2003). *Educating citizens: Preparing America's undergraduates for lives of moral and civic responsibility*. San Francisco, CA: Jossey-Bass.

Conrad, D., & Hedin, D. (1982). *Experiential education evaluation project*. St. Paul, MN: University of Minnesota.

Couto, R. A. (1982). *Streams of idealism and health care innovation: An assessment of service and learning and community mobilization*. New York, NY: Teachers College Press.

Cross, K. P. (1987). Review of problem-based learning in education for the professions. *Journal of Higher Education, 58*(4), 491.

Csikszentmihalyi, M., & Csikzentmihalyi, I. (1988). *Optimal experience: Psychological studies of flow in consciousness*. New York, NY: Cambridge University Press.

Csikzentmihaliy, M. (1990). *Flow: The psychology of optimal experience*. New York, NY: Harper and Row, Publishers.

Danzig, R., & Szanton, P. (1986). *National Service: What would it mean?* Lexington, MA: Lexington Books, D. C. Heath and Company.

Dewey, J. (1916). *Democracy and education: An introduction to the philosophy of education*. New York, NY: Macmillan, Inc.

Dewey, J. (1938). *Experience and education.* New York, NY: Simon and Schuster.

Duley, J. (1990, Fall). *The growth of experiential education in American secondary and post-secondary education: The role of NSIEE.* Raleigh, NC: The National Society of Internships and Experiential Education.

Edgerton, R. (1984). Abilities that last a lifetime: Alverno in perspective. *AAHE Bulletin, 36*(6).

Edwards, B., Foley, M., & Diani, M. (Eds.). (2001). *Beyond Tocqueville: Civil society and the social capital debate in comparative perspective.* Hanover, NH: University Press of New Hampshire.

Eyler, J., & Giles, D. E., Jr. (1999). *Where's the learning in service-learning?* San Francisco, CA: Jossey-Bass Publishers.

Fish, S. (2003, May 16). Aim low. *Chronicle of Higher Education*, p. C5.

Furgeson, A. (1995). *An essay on the history of civil society.* Cambridge, England: Cambridge University Press.

Gardner, J. (1984). Step one: Putting innovation into action. In First Annual You Can Make A Difference Conference—"Entrepreneurs in the Public Interest." Stanford, CA: Stanford University.

Giles, D., Honnet, E. P., & Migliore, S., (Eds.). (1991). *Research agenda for combining service and learning in the 1990s.* Raleigh, NC: National Society for Internships and Experiential Education.

Glasser, W. (1965) *Reality therapy—A new approach to psychiatry.* New York, NY: Harper & Row.

Goodlad, J. (1984). *A place called school: Prospects for the future.* New York, NY: McGraw-Hill.

Gramsci, A. (1971). *Selections from the prison notebooks.* New York, NY: International.

Harkavy, I. (2006) Engaged Scholarship, Engaged Teaching, and Engaged Learning: Penn's Faculty and Students in Partnership with Neighboring Communities. Haas Center Lecture on Public Service and the University, Stanford University, May 3, 2006.

Hamilton, S. F. (1981). Adolescents in community settings: What is to be learned? *Theory and Research in Social Education, 9*(2), 23–38.

Hamilton, S. F., & Frenzel, M. (1987, March). *The effect of volunteer service on early adolescents' social development.* Paper presented at the Annual AERA Conference, Washington, DC.

Harkavy, I. (2006). The role of universities in advancing citizenship and social justice in the 21st century. *Education, Citizenship, and Social Justice, 1*(1), 5–37.

Hegel, G. W. (1945). *The philosophy of right.* Oxford, England: Clarendon Press.

Honnet, E. P., & Poulsen. (1989). *Principles of good practice in combining service and learning. A Wingspread Special Report.* Racine, WI: The Johnson Foundation.

Joplin, L. (1995). On defining experiential education. In K. Warren, M. Sakofs, & J. S. Hunt, Jr. (Eds.), *The theory of experiential education* (pp. 15–22). Boulder, CO: Association for Experiential Education.

Jencks, C., & Riesman, D. (1968). *The academic revolution.* Garden City, NY: Doubleday.

Kahne, J., & Westheimer, J. (1996, May). In the service of what? The politics of service-learning. *Phi Delta Kappan 77*, 593–599.

Kaston, C. O., & Heffernan, J. (1984). *Preparing humanists for work: A national study of undergraduate internships in the humanities.* Washington, DC: National Endowment for the Humanities.

Kendall, J. C. and Associates (1990). *Combining service and learning: A resource book for community and public service, volume 1.* Raleigh, NC: National Society for Internships and Experiential Education.

Kendall, J. C., Duley, J. S., Little, T. C., Permaul, J. S., & Rubin, S. (1986). *Strengthening experiential education within your institution.* Raleigh, NC: National Society for Internships and Experiential Education.

Leming, J. (1993). Synthesis of research: In search of effective character education. *Educational Leadership, 51*(3), 63–71.

Levin, B. (2001). *Reforming education: From origins to outcomes.* New York, NY: Rutledge Falmer.

Loacker, G., Cromwell, L., & O'Brien (Ed.). (1986). *Assessment in higher education: To serve the learner.* Washington, DC: Office of Education Research and Improvement, USOE.

Luce, J., Anderson, J., Permaul, J., Shumer, R., Stanton, T., & Migliore, S. (1988). *Service-learning: An annotated bibliography.* Raleigh, NC: National Society for Internships and Experiential Education.

Melchior, A., & Bailis, L. (2002). Impact of service-learning on civic attitudes and behaviors of middle and high school youth: Findings from three national studies. In A. Furco & S. Billig (Eds.), *Service-learning: The essence of the pedagogy* (pp. 201–222). Greenwich, CT: Information Age.

McPherson, K., & Kinsley, C. W. (1995). *Enriching the curriculum through service learning.* Washington, DC: Association for Supervision and Curriculum Development.

National Commission on Resources for Youth. (n.d.). *Youth into adult: Towards a model for programs that facilitate the transition to adulthood.* New York, NY: National Commission on Resources for Youth.

National Commission on Resources for Youth. (1975, December). *Youth Participation: A Concept Paper.* A Report of the National Commission on Resources for Youth to the Department of Health, Education and Welfare, Office of Youth Development. New York, NY: National Commission on Resources for Youth.

National Institute of Education (1984). *Involvement in learning: Realizing the potential of American higher education.* Final Report of the Study Group on Conditions of Excellence in Higher Education. Washington, DC: National Institute of Higher Education.

Newman, F. (1985). *Higher education and the American Resurgence: A Carnegie Foundation Special Report.* Princeton, NJ: The Carnegie Foundation for the Advancement of Teaching.

Newmann, F., & Rutter, R. (1983). *The effects of high school community service programs on students' social development.* Madison, WI: Wisconsin Center for Education Research.

Owens, T. (1982). Experience-based career education: summary and implications of research and evaluation findings. *Child and Youth Services, 4*(3/4).

Parks Daloz, L. A., Keen, C. H., Keen, J. P., & Daloz Parks, S. (1996). *Common Fire: Leading Lives of Commitment in a Complex World.* Boston, MA: Beacon Press.

Permaul, J., Anderson, J., & Hughes, L. (1984). *Agenda for experiential education in the '80s.* PANEL Resource Paper #14. National Society for Internships and Experiential Education, Raleigh, NC. Peer Assistance Network in Experiential Learning.

Schine, J. (with B. Shoup & D. Harrington). (1981). *New roles for early adolescents.* New York, NY: The National Commission on Resources for Youth.

Schlecty, P. (1990). *Schools for the 21st century.* San Francisco, CA: Jossey-Bass.

Shumer, R. (1993). *Describing service-learning: A Delphi study.* Department of Vocational and Technical Education, College of Education, University of Minnesota, Minneapolis.

Sigmon, R (1979, Spring). Service-learning: Three principles. National Center for Service-Learning, ACTION. *Synergist, 8*(1), 9–11.

Sizer, T. (1984). *Horace's compromise: The dilemma of the American high school.* New York, NY: Houghton Mifflin Company.

Sizer, T (1992). *Horace's school.* New York, NY: Houghton Mifflin Company.

Skinner, R., & Chapman, C. (1999). *Service-learning and community service in K–12 public schools. Statistics in brief.* Rockville, MD: Westat.

Smith, D., & Theophano, J. (1976). *The Academy for Career Education: An ethnographic evaluation, External evaluator's final report on the EBCE programs. Volume IV.* Berkeley, CA: Educational Testing Service.

Spotts, R., & Evenson, J. (1977). *Experience-based career education—Evaluation of outcomes at three pilot programs, 1976–77.* Berkeley, CA: Far West Laboratory for Educational Research and Development.

Stanton, T. (1990). Service-learning: Groping toward a definition. In J. Kendall & Associates (Eds.), *Combining service and learning: A resource book for community and public service* (pp. 65–67). Raleigh, NC: National Society for Internships and Experiential Education.

Stanton, T. K. (1988, January). *Linking service to the curriculum: The faculty role.* Proceedings of the Campus Compact National Meeting, Washington, DC.

Stanton, T. (1990a). Liberal arts, experiential learning and public service: Necessary ingredients for socially responsible undergraduate education. In J. C. Kendall (Ed.), *Combining service and learning: A resource book for public and community service* (pp. 175–189). Raleigh, NC: National Society for Internships and Experiential Education.

Stanton, T. K. (1990b). *Integrating public service with academic study: The faculty role. (A Campus Compact report).* Denver, CO: Education Commission of the States.

Stanton, T., Giles, D., & Cruz, N. (1999). *Service-learning: A movement's pioneers reflect on its origins, practice, and future.* San Francisco, CA: Jossey-Bass.

Toqueville, A. (1835/1968). *Democracy in America.* London, England: Fontana.

Wagner, J. (1986). *Academic excellence and community service through experiential education: Encouraging students to teach.* Keynote presentation to Ninth Annual University of California Conference on Experiential Learning. Available as NSIEE Occasional Paper, National Society for Internships and Experiential Education, Raleigh, NC.

Waring, A. L. (1988) *Dissertation proposal.* Stanford University, Stanford, CA.

Warren, K., Sakoffs, M., & Hunt, J. (1995). *The theory of experiential education.* Dubuque, IA: Kendal Hunt.

Waterman, A. (1997). *Service-learning: Applications from the research.* Mahwah, NJ: Earlbaum.

William T. Grant Foundation on Work, Family, and Citizenship (1988). *The forgotten half: Non-college youth in America.* Washington, DC: Author.

CHAPTER 2

THE WISDOM
OF JOHN DULEY

John Duley

Wisdom: By wisdom in this chapter we are looking for principles and practices about learning that have withstood the test of time and have provided approaches that have proven their worth in empowering ordinary people to accomplish extraordinary things in the realms of social justice and making the world a more humane place in which to live. I believe that Service Learning at its best contains this wisdom. So then, if you believe or would like to believe that Service Learning has the capability to empower people to live a life for the common good, then read on.

I have chosen to use the Michigan State University (MSU)/Rust College Student Tutorial Education Project (STEP) because it is the only project in which a longitudinal study of the impact of service-learning on the participants has been done (Duley, 2012). This study was begun in preparation for a reunion of its participants in a conference hosted at MSU by President Lou Anna K. Simon on the weekend of Dr. Martin Luther King, Jr.'s birthday in 2007—40 years after the project was completed in 1968. Following the STEP program, I used the same insights and practices gained from that project during my tenure as director of the required semester-long "off campus cross cultural" program at Justin

Where's the Wisdom in Service-Learning?, pages 33–43
Copyright © 2017 by Information Age Publishing
All rights of reproduction in any form reserved.

Morrill College at MSU and in my work as an educational consultant to MSU faculty members engaging their students in experiential learning.

During the summer months of 1965–68, 97 student volunteers and 10 faculty members from Michigan State University volunteered in a service-learning project at Rust College, a small African American liberal arts college in Holly Springs, Mississippi. The college was founded by the Freedman's Aid Society of the Methodist Episcopal Church in 1866 and celebrated its 145th commencement ceremony in May 2011. Like many colleges, Rust adheres to the three pillars of education: teaching, research, and community service.

This project, called STEP, was the result of a phone call from a student of Professor Robert L. Green, Mary Ann Shupenko, who had participated in Freedom Summer and had dropped out of school to continue to work with of the Council of Confederated Organizations in Canton, Mississippi. She was a close personal friend of the Green family and called Green to keep him abreast of what was happening in Mississippi. She invited him to participate in a voter registration rally with James Farmer, the director of the Council on Racial Equality in Canton. Green was then a professor of education at MSU and I was the University Presbyterian Chaplin. Green called me, and we went.

While participating in this event, and feeling that Michigan State University should be making some educational contribution to the Movement, Green and I sought to ascertain which Black colleges were in trouble with their boards of trustees or the state because of the involvement of their students and faculty in the Civil Rights movement. The name Rust College kept being mentioned. On our return to Michigan State, we recruited two students, Laura Lichlighter, a member of the All University Student government, and Frank Bianco, a graduate student in charge of the Student Education Corps, to accompany us on a visit to Rust College. As a result of that visit we were invited by Rust President Earnest Smith and Rust Academic Dean William McMillan to develop and bring the STEP program to the college as a service-learning project.

SERVICE-LEARNING AND LIVING
FOR THE COMMON GOOD

This chapter is not about how people gain new knowledge through experience. It is about how ordinary people can accomplish extraordinary things. Berkowitz's (1987) answer is that "it is because of their values, things that are latent in all of us" (pp. 322–323). One's involvement in creating a more just and humane world has to do with the affective domain.

David Kolb's (1984) excellent experiential learning theory, which has to do with the cognitive domain, has helped us establish our place in the academy. He has shown us, and the skeptics, how people acquire the coin of the academy—assessable knowledge, through experience. But, this article is not about cognitive learning, it is about the pedagogy of engagement.

In 1997, Dr. Russell Edgerton, Director of the Pew Charitable Trust, delivered "a White Paper to the American Association of Higher Education" in which he spelled out the problems confronting higher education and what his agency would commit their resources to. In that paper he characterized the dominant mode of teaching and learning in higher education as "teaching and telling"—learning by recall. He made the significant point:

> That mode of instruction fails to help students acquire two kinds of learning that are now crucial to their individual success and critically needed by our society at large. The first is real understanding. The second is "habits of the heart" that motivate students to be caring citizens. Both of these qualities are acquired through pedagogues that elicit intense engagement.... To be a citizen one must not only be informed. One must also care, and be willing to act on one's values and ideas. Crucial to all the new civic literacies is the development of an emotional identification with the larger community and the belief that, in the face of overwhelming complexity, one individual can make a difference.... How do we learn such "habits of the heart"'...? The complete answer is complicated, but the quick answer is that students acquire habits of the heart in situations in which they are intensely and emotionally engaged: not just reading a play but acting in it; not just reading about the homeless, but working in a soup kitchen or homeless shelter, and reflecting on what they have experienced. (Edgerton, 1997, p. 35)

Another voice of wisdom was that of Dr. Lee Shulman. In a 2002 paper entitled "Making Differences: A Table of Learning," Shulman pointed out that despite Bloom's taxonomy of cognitive domain, little attention was paid to the affective domain until the taxonomy developed by Krathwohl, Bloom, and Masia (1968). Shulman goes on to describe the taxonomy of the affective domain:

> It depicts how learners move from a willingness to receive an experience, to begin to respond to it, to value what is taught, to organize it within their larger set of values and attitudes, and ultimately to internalize those values such that they no longer need an external stimulus to trigger the associated affective and emotional responses. (Shulman, 2002, p. 36)

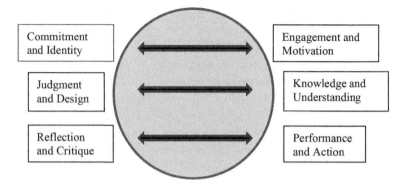

Figure 2.1 Table of Learning. *Source:* Adapted from Shulman, 2002, p. 42.

Knowing the value of taxonomies, Shulman created the Table of Learning as a taxonomy for a pedagogy of engagement.(see Figure 2.1). According to Shulman,

> the taxonomy makes the following assertion: Learning begins with student engagement, which in turn leads to knowledge and understanding. Once someone understands, he or she becomes capable of performance or action. Critical reflection on one's practice and understanding leads to higher-order thinking in the form of a capacity to exercise judgment in the face of uncertainty and to create designs in the presence of constraints and unpredictability. Ultimately, the exercise of judgment makes possible the development of commitment. In commitment, we become capable of professing our understandings and our values, our faith and our love, our skepticism and our doubts, internalizing those attributes and making them integral to our identities. These commitments, in turn, make new engagements possible—and even necessary. (Shulman, 2002, p. 38)

STEP, THE PEDAGOGIES OF ENGAGEMENT, AND THE AFFECTIVE DOMAIN

What qualifies STEP as a pedagogy of engagement? It was a collaborative, project-based service-learning program whose purposes were determined by the agency being served, qualities defined by Edgerton (1997). During the visit to Rust College by Robert Green, Laura Leichliter, Frank Bianco, and this author in November 1964, an invitation was extended to MSU by Rust College President Ernest Smith and Academic Dean William McMillan. The purpose of the invitation was to accomplish three things: (a) to better prepare Mississippi African American high school graduates for the college level curriculum at Rust College, (b) to help Rust College obtain its accreditation, and (c) to provide a community recreation and cultural program for 11- to 14-year-olds. To address these needs, MSU student and faculty leaders worked with Rust advisors to develop a program in which MSU students would provide remedial courses in math, science, writing, reading, social science, communication, and study skills for all entering freshman in a 5 week residential program at the college; MSU faulty & library science people would teach summer courses and work to upgrade the library; and volunteers, with the help of the director of MSU's Intermural Program, Dr. Frank Beaman, would lead a cultural recreation program for all adolescents in Marshall County. Thus STEP was born.

THE COLLABORATIVE NATURE WITHIN STEP

This service-leaning project was collaborative on several levels, both within MSU and between MSU and Rust College. Collaboration also took place between and among students, faculty, and administration at both schools. Several of the participants in the 2007 reunion and study discussed this aspect of the project. Some recalled the sense of ownership that cooperative involvement in all levels of the project gave them.

Kay Snyder, Class of 1967

> There was a group of us; we knew many of the people who were setting STEP up. These leaders involved a number of us from the very early stages of the planning. So I think this program was something that had a real impact on my life; it was to be taken seriously, working with faculty who were committed to civil rights. They were committed to something big, and being involved in the various steps of this gave me a real sense of ownership. Today, when I was hearing again the speech that Martin Luther King Jr. gave here at MSU in '65 launching this program, I realized that STEP was transformative in my life.

Others mentioned the continuity of their commitment to the program and the personal nature of their engagement with the project.

Linda Garcia Shelton, Class of 1968

> I was involved right from the beginning; I was in the first group in '65, and I was again in '66 . . . Then in the '67 year I was involved in raising money and setting it up, but I did not go.

In 1965 Linda met Harold Shelton, who was also a STEP participant, and they were married in the spring of '66. They spent their honeymoon that summer working in STEP.

William Skocpol, Class of 1968

> About three weeks into the 1966 session, I noticed another volunteer. We were both students at Michigan State, but with 40,000 students we probably wouldn't have met, so we rapidly took great notice of each other, and fell in love. We spent the next year as leaders of some aspects of the 1967 program. I coordinated the people who were developing curriculum and teaching skills for math, and Theda did that for communication skills. On the sort of educational side of things we had those roles, and by the end of the year we got married on June 10th and then went down on June 17th to oversee the beginning of the program and then return to East Lansing.

William's wife Theda later became the dean of Graduate Programs at Harvard and, as a result of the same values she honed in her STEP experience, sought there to ensure the inclusion of people of color to the graduate student body.

COLLABORATION BETWEEN MSU AND RUST COLLEGE

Collaboration, which Edgerton indicated was of great importance, also existed at all levels among the people of MSU and Rust College. In the early days of STEP, Rust Dean McMillan came to MSU, and recruited, with the help of Richard Chapin, Head MSU Librarian, a Library Science student, Bill Nelton, to go to Rust for the Spring Quarter of 1965 to begin work on up-grading the libraries. Dean McMillian also advised students about Mississippi mores. Eddie Smith, Business Manager for Rust College, and other staff members participated in the subsequent Spring Planning Retreats. Faculty from MSU conducted summer classes for the local segregated public school teachers. These MSU PhDs also added to the number of required PhD professors for Rust to become an accredited college. Rust College student, Paul Herron, was in the STEP program in 1966, and came to MSU in 1967 to work in the Linney Lab. He lived with STEP student leaders, helped recruit STEP volunteers, and ended up staying on to gain his PhD. Herron was the initiator of the 2007 study of STEP participants.

THE AFFECTIVE DOMAIN AND THE INSIGHTS PROVIDED BY SHULMAN'S TABLE OF TEACHING

The 12 participants of the 2007 STEP interviews identified ten of the same values and characteristics revealed by the participants in the in-depth studies conducted by Berkowitz in *Local Heroes: The Rebirth of Heroism in America* (1987) and Daloz, Keen, Keen, and Parks (1996) in *Common Fire: Lives of Commitment in a Complex World* (see Table 2.1).

THE AFFECTIVE DOMAIN AND STEP

The following quotations and summaries of the interviews with the STEP participants illustrate the intense engagement of the students as well as the development of understanding, reflection, the exercise of judgment, and the establishment of identity (commitment). One of the students expressed the revelation that all that is wrong is not just present in Mississippi. She struggled with her idealism and naïveté, but involvement in the STEP project led her to discover her life's work.

Kay Snyder, Class of 1967

I want to say something about the moral issue. And that is, I look...at my journal and I realize there was this moral issue that needed to be addressed, a transformation taking place, but what I also realized repeatedly, from the students that we worked with and subsequent involvements, that...for whites from the North to go down and think, "Oh Mississippi, they have such a problem and we need to help with this problem," was really very presumptuous and very ethnocentric. What I often realized is that for blacks in Mississippi at that time, this was their home and for us to come...and put-down their state almost viciously, was offensive. I came back to the North...to my own situations, to realize what kinds of inequalities existed. I knew about them, but it wasn't so black and white. There were many things that we needed to do but

TABLE 2.1 The Affective Domain	
Values	**Characteristics**
• Belief in the power of one person to make a difference • Willingness to take personal risks • Belief in hard work and that it pays off • Spirituality • Compassion "do the right thing"	• Naïveté • Living within a tribe and the ability to break tribal barriers • Persistence, perseverance, resilience • Experienced marginality as a factor in the development of compassion

that weren't being done in the North, and there were many issues involving not just race but gender, and social class as well. And so it was a . . . humbling experience. They (the Rust College students) wanted us to be mindful of what we were saying to them, and that sometimes we were more concerned with changing the society than dealing with their issues. So looking at my adult life, not only did I become a college professor but, also I teach sociology, and my area of interest is equalities, and I now teach a lot about gender in sociology. The sociology of gender . . . wasn't even a topic then; I never studied it in graduate school It certainly wasn't an issue at that time, but it was the undercurrent of realizing, now, wait a minute, wait a minute, if we're going to talk about justice and inequality, hmm . . . it isn't just in one domain. We have to think what if, what's happening to women. The seeds of all of this were planted in the work of the STEP Project.

Discovering that the things "wrong" in Mississippi shed light on the things "wrong" at home changed this participant's world view and helped her to see areas in her own community where work needed to be done. The next participant continued to actively live out the values shaped and expressed in the STEP program.

Merrie Milton, Class of 1967

After graduation, Milton moved to South Carolina to teach third grade and support integration. By non-violent direct-action she, with others, forced a store serving mostly African Americans to hire Black clerks and a radio station advertising to African Americans to replace a White disc jockey with an African American. Because of these involvements her job contract was not renewed. She returned to Detroit's inner-city to teach a class of 35 African American and Latino first grade children in a very difficult educational environment for 20 years, retiring only because of a serious health problem. For Milton, her work in STEP became a defining factor in the establishment of her identity and personal integrity. She, along with the next participant, embodied this integrity even in the face of difficult and sometimes dangerous circumstances.

Christine Lundberg, Class of 1966

After the 1966 STEP project she taught for two years at Rust College, then taught in a Black high school in Drew, Mississippi where she met Fannie Lou Hamer and participated in many marches for racial justice with her. Her job contract was terminated at the end of the second year because of her non-violent direct-action in support of African American employment. She moved to Jackson, Mississippi and worked for Head Start for 5 years, becoming involved with the NAACP Defense Fund. She moved on to Washington, DC, participated in many protests for social justice and now directs as Small Business Development Program in Martinsburg, West Virginia helping African Americans start their own businesses.

These three participants all exemplify key values and characteristics outlined above. The values and characteristics fostered and solidified by their involvement in STEP led them to lives committed to making the world a more humane place in which to live, and even to risking their lives to establish justice.

Risk taking, belief in doing the right thing, belief that one person can make a difference, and commitment are revealed by the following participants.

John Schuiteman, Class of 1966

An Air Force ROTC MSU graduate awaiting assignment in Vietnam, Schuiteman came from a relatively conservative background. Teaching at Rust and participating in the last day of the March Against Fear, led him to get a PhD in and teach Political Science, to become pro-active in marching for Gay Rights and, as a Vietnam veteran, protesting against the war in Iraq. Speaking out when others remained silent became for him "the right thing to do," and STEP gave him the courage of his commitments.

David Hollister, Graduate Class of 1968

Despite the acknowledged risks, he and his family chose to spend two summers in the STEP program. Because of his opposition to the war in Vietnam, he was considering emigrating to Canada, but as a result of the meeting with Dr. King and his participation in STEP, Hollister chose to go into public service. He successfully ran for the office of County Commissioner, served 19 years in the Michigan House of Representatives, ten years as Mayor of the City of Lansing, and currently serves as the Director of the Primas Civitas Foundation, bringing new businesses into the Lansing area.

THE RELATIONSHIP BETWEEN SERVICE-LEARNING AND THE SCHOLARSHIP OF ENGAGEMENT

There is a developing movement within higher education, the scholarship of engagement, in which researchers go to the community to learn from them what their needs are rather than bringing them the results of research that has nothing to do with their concerns. The emphasis is then upon the needs of the community rather than on the dictates of the academy. Faculty seek to do what Linda Garcia Shelton describes as her work,

> My community involvement stems from my work. I have worked with a community-based umbrella organization to develop plans for a multidisciplinary health care clinic that has services the community defined as important to them. The plans also include health professionals' education within the sites, as well as a health research program that is driven by the community's definition of what they need to know, not the university's definition of what is important to study.

The scholarship of engagement comes to focus on service rather than on academic glory. STEP alum Caroline Wong's leadership style is an expression of this new movement.

> As a leader I look to a lot of other leaders to see what type of leader I want to be, and I really would define myself as a servant leader. I'm here to live, but I'm also here to serve you and serve your needs, and that concept was intrinsic to the Holly Springs experience. We were there not because we had something more or something better, but we were there to walk beside people and live with them and share with them and be of service to them to meet their needs.

CONCLUSION

In the foregoing pages we have explored the "pedagogies of engagement" of Russell Edgerton (1997) and Lee Shulman's (2002) "Table of Learnings." In so doing, we have confirmed the primacy of the affective domain, and the importance of Shulman's (2002) Table of Learning, for the purposes of value clarification, and personal and character development, as opposed to David Kolb's (1984) learning theory, which focuses on the cognitive domain exclusively.

The four conclusions of this study are:

1. Service-Learning and Civic Engagement can be life transforming, leading people to "do justice" and "work to create a more humane world;" and thus to work for "The Common Good."
2. The affective domain is the key to living for the common good. Therefore, we must encourage deep and searching reflection by participants, asking such questions such as, "What does this experience tell me about what is important to me? What is it I value?

What does it say about who I am? What is worthy of the investment of my life? What does it tell me about how I understand and view the world?"

3. Because it is the affective domain of learning that contributes to personal and character development, leading to living for the common good, we must plan, develop, implement, and evaluate our programs to include as many aspects of the pedagogies of engagement as possible, and use the Table of Learning as the overarching framework for our programs to make sure we are not exploiting communities.

4. We must relate our work to the scholarship of engagement as an outgrowth of, and parallel development to, the service-learning movement in order to be fully engaged in the academy and the community in doing justice and creating a more humane world.

REFERENCES

Berkowitz, W. R. (1987). *Local heroes: The rebirth of heroism in America*. Lexington, MA: Lexington Books.

Daloz, L. A. P., Keen, C. H., Keen, J. P., & Parks, S. D. (1996). *Common fire: Lives of commitment in a complex world*. Boston, MA: Beacon Press.

Duley, J. (2012). Service-learning and civic engagement as preparation for a life committed to working for the common good: An analysis of the Michigan State University-Rust College Student Tutorial Education Project 1965–1968. In H. E. Fitzgerald (Ed.), *Going public: Civic and community engagement, the scholarship of practice* (pp. 107–127), East Lansing: Michigan State University Press.

Edgerton, R. (1997). *Education white paper*. Report for the Pew Charitable Trust Board of Directors.

Kolb, D. A. (1984). *Experiential Learning*. Englewood Cliffs, NJ: Prentice Hall.

Krathwohl, D. R., Bloom, B. S., & Masia, B. B. (1968). *Taxonomy of educational objectives, the classification of educational goals. Handbook II: Affective Domain*. New York, NY: David McKay.

Shulman, L. (2002). Making differences: A table of learning. *Change: The Magazine of Higher Learning, 34*(6), 36–44.

CHAPTER 3

SERVICE LEARNING

Memories and Perspectives

William R. Ramsay

Service-Learning is defined in various ways by those who are involved in programs that relate acts of service to conscious learning. The phrase was coined in late 1966 or early 1967 in my office at Oak Ridge Associated Universities (ORAU) in Oak Ridge, Tennessee to describe internships first sponsored by the Tennessee Valley Authority (TVA) and administered by ORAU in 1964. Students and faculty involved came from the University of Tennessee. By the spring of 1967 the program, having grown to include other sponsoring agencies and areas, moved to the Southern Regional Education Board in Atlanta, Georgia.

A SIMPLE DEFINITION

The simple definition of service-learning is the linking of the performance of a needed community service to conscious reflection on the experience and relating it to other learning. The service is not contrived or arranged

Where's the Wisdom in Service-Learning?, pages 45–66
Copyright © 2017 by Information Age Publishing
All rights of reproduction in any form reserved.

from an academic setting, as in "field study," but is meeting a real need defined by a community service organization. The learning component may have a campus base or be structured in the experience at the agency with time for reflection and critical thinking. It may or may not involve academic credit and may be paid or unpaid depending on the circumstances. Generally, the service is not simply applying classroom learning to a real life setting, but rather relating what is learned from the experience to what has been learned in the classroom and library for increased knowledge and understanding. Ideally, the service setting is a learning laboratory available to students and, through them, the college or university would gain greater knowledge and insights, having an impact on what is taught.

The phrase "service-learning" is used to emphasize the positive value component of the service, rather than the value neutral "field experience education" or "experiential learning." Service-learning adds a discipline of "usefulness" or "contribution" to the student experience. Some other forms of experiential learning tend to be career and curriculum specific. Cooperative education is well established as an effective component of engineering and business education programs. Practice teaching is part of teacher education. Clinical experience and internships are part of medical professional education. Service-learning is a way of thinking and acting that links one's service to a community, with reflecting on the experiences in a conscious and disciplined way. It is a pattern for lifelong learning.

The linking of service and learning did not originate with the phrase service-learning, and there are many manifestations of this phenomenon in the past and at present. The program that gave rise to the phrase had its roots in the Oak Ridge Institute of Nuclear Studies and Tennessee Valley Authority. My story of how this came about is necessarily autobiographical to some extent and does not pretend to include other stories of those who were involved nor of those who came to apply the phrase service-learning to their various programs.

THE PATH TO SERVICE-LEARNING

It happened in Oak Ridge, Tennessee at Oak Ridge Associated Universities, formerly known as Oak Ridge Institute of Nuclear Studies. It was not nuclear science itself that gave rise to the service-learning program back in the 1960s but rather experience with some of the programs that had developed to meet a need for relationships between higher education and the post-war atomic energy program. Much of the research, development, and technology of nuclear science had taken place during the years of World War II as a carefully guarded secret under the name, The Manhattan Project. National laboratories, production and testing facilities had been created across the country at places such as the University of Chicago, Hanford, Washington, Los Alamos, New Mexico, Brookhaven on Long Island, New York and Oak Ridge, Tennessee. The existence and purpose of these widespread facilities was dramatically thrust onto the world stage with the atomic bomb and the end of the war. The world would never be the same. The story of this epic adventure is told in various places. But what happened after this climax?

Much of the attention of the national laboratories and related facilities after the war was turned to the peaceful potential of atomic energy in industry, in agriculture, in medicine and in power production. University scientists had been a very important part of the war effort and were returning to their institutions, but their services were still needed in the new applications. Furthermore they returned to institutions with no equipment close to that at the national laboratories and with the need to update curricula to reflect the new science. University and college students, teachers and researchers were needed by the laboratories and, in turn, they needed access to the laboratories for their equipment and expertise. A bridge was needed to permit and encourage two-way traffic between higher education and the atomic energy program. The Atomic Energy Commission established a series of programs to accomplish this and provided support for a group of universities to form an organization to develop and administer these programs. The organization was called the Oak Ridge Institute of Nuclear Studies (ORINS) with headquarters near the Oak Ridge National Laboratory.

ORINS was a nonprofit corporation of all the major Southern universities with a council of university scientists who selected a board of directors made up primarily of university presidents, vice-presidents, and deans. One of the leaders of the effort was named executive director—William G. Pollard, formerly a physicist at Rice University. ORINS offered seminars and conferences during periods of research in the national laboratories for university scientists and graduate fellowships with internships at the laboratories. It developed and operated a Medical Division which engaged in clinical research on nuclear medicine at a hospital in Oak Ridge. ORINS also offered special training programs in the uses of radioisotopes for scientists and technicians from industry, agriculture, and medicine, and it built and operated the nation's Museum of Atomic Energy with related outreach programs of traveling exhibits and teaching for communities and high schools throughout the country.

Having a strong sense of public service and diligence in the use of public funds, ORINS, along with the Tennessee Valley Authority, state governments, and universities, participated in a graduate program in public administration—The Southern Regional Training Program in Public Administration. This program, organized after World War II, required an internship and then graduate courses at the universities of Alabama,

Tennessee, and Kentucky, all in one year! The program was motivated by a desire to develop professional administrators for public service to replace the old spoils system that still plagued much of the South. I was fortunate to be awarded one of these fellowships upon graduation from Berea College and was assigned for my internship in the summer of 1952 to the Oak Ridge Institute of Nuclear Studies.

After I completed my internship and married my college sweetheart, Rose Moore, on September 7, 1952, we planned to move to Tuscaloosa, Alabama to begin graduate study at the university. But the military draft intervened and 1 month and a day after our wedding I reported to Fort Jackson, South Carolina to begin training and duty in the U.S. Army Medical Corps. This was during the Korean War when all young men were subject to the draft. My request for an educational deferment was denied by my rural Georgia draft board whose members thought that 4 years of college was already more education than was really needed. After basic training, I was sent to Fort Sam Houston in Texas for x-ray training. I think my summer at Oak Ridge triggered the assumption that I was a good candidate for training in anything related to radiation. By the time I completed my 2 years of service I was not only an x-ray technician, who could name all the bones of the body, but had become father of a son.

The Southern Regional Training Program graciously let me pick up with studies at the University of Alabama in the fall of 1954 where I joined a group of five other fellows. By Christmas, we finished the semester at Alabama and moved on to Tennessee, with the addition of a baby girl. In the spring, we finished the term at Tennessee and moved on to the last semester at Kentucky. The Veterans Administration was thoroughly confused by all this changing of schools and stopped my benefits for several months. We became heavily identified with poverty. But there was light at the end of the tunnel. The VA finally got things straightened out and we received all our past benefits at once just before the program ended. I had been offered a position upon graduation at the Oak Ridge Institute of Nuclear Studies. We moved to Oak Ridge in the summer of 1955 where I began duties as administrative assistant in the University Relations Division.

By the 1960s I had moved into positions in central administration responsible for personnel services, legal services, and a variety of administrative services. Several of us in administration belonged to the American Society for Public Administration. We periodically met in Knoxville with colleagues from the TVA and the University of Tennessee to discuss professional matters, public policy, and politics. The whole civil rights struggle was an exciting time to be involved in public service in the South and national attention was turning to other social issues, especially in places like Appalachia where we were. President Kennedy had called on citizens to give of themselves in service to our country, and to other nations, in all kinds of ways. He established the Peace Corps and other service agencies. Our little discussion group talked about what might be done in our area for the benefit of our communities. Paul Elza and Wendell Russell of ORINS, along with myself; Bob Lowry, Bob Krapf, and Ted Schultz of TVA; and Buck Buchanan of the University of Tennessee were regular participants in such discussions.

Although President Johnson would not declare the War on Poverty until his 1965 state of the union message, things were already happening to foster community development and economic improvement. The Tennessee Valley Authority had established a "Tributary Area Development" program involving local people in areas defined by river valleys in finding ways to improve opportunities and services in their communities. Some of us in Oak Ridge became involved in the Clinch and Powell River Valley Association under this TVA program. One of the first tasks was to determine what was already in place and what needs were not being met. We began to talk to county and city officials, school personnel, industrial leaders, and citizens about possibilities. What manpower needs and opportunities did business and industry have? What training programs were available? What were the problems in the schools? What natural resources were available? What opportunities were there for cultural and recreational activities? What about the area's infrastructure? It was obvious that a lot of work needed to be done just to get to a planning stage.

Meanwhile, ORINS was seeking ways to contribute to the new push for resource and community development. With a grant from the Department of Labor, it published a report entitled "Manpower for Development," suggesting ways to better train and utilize human resources based on what was learned about relating higher education with the atomic energy program. The report called for upgrading vocational training using the high technology of Oak Ridge. It suggested other ways to mobilize the resources of education, industry, and government in the area for development. Recommendations included internships with community service and development agencies involving students and faculty both to contribute and to learn. With the cooperation of the Atomic Energy Commission, University of Tennessee, and Union Carbide Corporation (the operator of the Oak Ridge National Laboratory and the production plants), ORINS organized a training program for unemployed or underemployed persons. The training was situated in the middle of one of the high tech production areas at the Y-12 plant with access to sophisticated equipment and expertise. It was a hybrid of apprenticeship and institutional training at a very high level. For example, welding was taught with space age specifications rather than the typical machine shop standards. Graduates were highly employable and leapt into high paying jobs.

The idea of using local development agencies and community service programs as "laboratories" in which students could both contribute and learn continued to be explored. TVA came up with some funds to start an experimental program with the Clinch Powell River Valley Association that would place student interns at the disposal of Clinch and Powell River Valley Association to carry out some of its research. ORINS agreed to administer the programs and the University of Tennessee provided the educational connection. Four interns were selected from the University of Tennessee and each was given an assignment in a different county in the region. Each intern was provided a committee which was composed of a local sponsor (such as a county executive), a university professor, and a technical resource person. The committee was not supervisory and may not even meet, but rather it represented points of access and assistance for the intern. The intern was to use the committee rather than the other way around. It took a while for the students to adjust to this new posture. Their projects had been designed by the agency with help from ORINS. TVA provided the technical assistance person. A professor from the University of Tennessee was selected to help with research resources, quality of reporting and documentation, and to assist in setting and assessing learning objectives and outcomes. Whether or not the student received academic credit depended on his situation and the policies of the university. Academic credit and learning were not considered synonymous. Each intern was to prepare a comprehensive report, in good form and properly documented, which was then published by ORINS and given to the agency. For the students, it introduced a new discipline of "usefulness," as well as scholarship, to their research and reporting. One intern observed, "The way I write this report will determine not only whether I get an 'A' or 'B' but will have an effect on people's lives!"

The first four internships in 1964 were so successful that funds were secured by TVA and ORINS to have more in 1965. One of the first four interns compiled a list of the various federal programs and grants available to Campbell County, Tennessee. He collected information from the various arms of the departments of Agriculture, Education, Commerce, Labor, and other agencies. He did such a thorough job that the report became a "best seller" beyond Campbell County, especially in Washington, and served as the first listing of what became the "yellow pages" of federal programs. It also brought the internship program to the attention of many agencies. It became clear that the program had great potential and would spread beyond TVA and the East Tennessee area. TVA encouraged contact with other agencies to expand the program. By the time the second group of interns' work had been completed, there was support for the following year from the Economic Development Administration, Office of Economic Opportunity, and other federal and state agencies.

I had been given leave from my regular administrative duties to pursue and coordinate the new programs of "resource development" at ORINS, including the internships. As we moved into a much larger scale program covering a wider area, more staff was needed. In addition to liaison with supporting agencies, internships needed to be developed with local sponsors, universities needed to be visited to find interested faculty and students. My brother, Dick, suggested I get in touch with a colleague of his who worked with the American Friends Service Committee College program, getting students involved in service projects. So, Bob Sigmon came for an interview and it was clear that he was the man for the job. He caught the vision, but it took some doing to convince him that it was not a moral wrong to accept a decent salary for doing something worthwhile. I think his wife, Marian, was on my side.

With Bob's good services we soon had internships set up in several states for the summer of 1966 with economic development and community service agencies, and it looked like the program would quickly expand further. Agencies were eager for the help of motivated, bright students, and outward looking teachers were seeking opportunities to be involved. Sponsorship was growing and local participation in cost-sharing allowed even faster growth. Another staff member, Mike Hart from Tennessee, was added. However, because of the rapid growth, problems were developing in the ORINS governance structure. ORINS was changing its name to Oak Ridge Associated Universities (ORAU), and attention was drawn to what its purpose and priorities should be.

The ORAU Board of Directors was strongly supportive of the new resource development initiatives but the larger Council had some unease, and even hostility in the case of a few members. The Council, made up entirely of university scientists, had misgivings about getting away from a science focus and into the messy social issues of the day. Although the name changed that year from ORINS to ORAU, it was still a science orientated organization. Leadership on the Board saw an opportunity to strengthen the internship program by moving it to a base with more political involvement, more conducive to public policy matters. Many of the same university presidents on the ORAU board were also involved in the Southern Regional Education Board (SREB), with headquarters in Atlanta, and decided that would be a better location for the internship program. The training programs based in the Oak Ridge facilities and other activities directly serving the local area were to stay at ORAU.

SREB is an interstate compact with all southern states represented: each by the governor, two legislators and two university representatives. Visionary leaders had formed it after WWII to upgrade higher education in the region by sharing resources, and it had been very successful. It has a reputation for careful policy development, scholarly meetings, and publications. It helped develop the community college idea and implementation, provided leadership in improvements in mental health care and training, fostered growth in nursing education, and made positive contributions in other areas of higher education and public policy. The internship program was a good fit, although at the time there was some apprehension about getting involved in actual social and developmental services. I was given the opportunity to move the program to SREB in the midst of its activity and growth. So in the spring of 1967 we moved, with our five children, to Atlanta, Georgia.

Before the move to Atlanta, we had a meeting in my office to discuss, among other things, what to call this arrangement we were promoting between agencies and educational institutions. Bob Sigmon was there, and I think Wendell Russell of ORAU. My memory is not clear as to whether Mike Hart was there or came on board later. We were familiar with cooperative education, field experience programs, practice teaching and other useful devices for linking education and experience, but none seemed to fit. We considered "experiential learning," "action-learning," and other combinations but finally settled on "service-learning," because it implied a value dimension that best described what we were trying to do. The hyphen in service-learning was considered to be very important, suggesting a mutually supportive balance between providing a service and thinking about it in a disciplined way. So we began to refer to the internships as service-learning.

After the move to Atlanta we included Donald Eberly in some of our deliberations and consultations. We asked him to do an evaluation of the program from his perspective as founder of the National Service Secretariat. Don, a graduate of Harvard and MIT, wasn't sure the phrase service-learning was erudite enough. As he reports in his book, *National Service: A Promise to Keep* (Eberly, 1988),

> It was a superbly designed operation and I said so in my report. About the only flaw I could see was the use of "service-learning" as a descriptor. If the idea was to gain the currency it deserved, I thought it needed a livelier name. (p. 55)

Don consulted a friend who was a Greek scholar and came up with the phrase "Diakonia-Paedia," and used that name in his report. We, of course, asked Don to interpret it for us. He explained that the word "diakonia" means community with a service connotation, as in deacon—a person who serves the community. "Paedia," he said had the same root as "pedagogy" or teaching. Thus, it meant community service as a teacher, or "service-learning." We suggested that not everyone had the benefits of Harvard and MIT educations and it would be hard to understand, and not to mention, pronounce. In his book, written years later, Don observes: "I haven't seen a reference to 'Diakonia-Paedia' since then, but 'service-learning' soon became a fairly common term on the nation's campuses" (Eberly, 1988, p. 55).

And now, 50 years later, the phrase service-learning is commonly used throughout the country to describe programs linking community service with learning goals and outcomes. The phrase means somewhat different things to different people. To some, it is primarily a service program, with attendant learning acknowledged. Others see it primarily as an educational technique using a community service setting to meet an academic requirement. I prefer to think of it as a way of thinking and of living. A life of service in whatever setting and a mind alive with questions and new learning from experience is full and satisfying.

SOME EARLY EXPERIENCES AND EXAMPLES

Early in our experiences at ORAU and SREB we learned some important lessons. First we found other programs that had arisen in other areas, like the Urban Corp, which connected us with kindred spirits like Michael Goldstein. We began to have conferences and meetings to explore mutual interests and interact with governmental agencies and universities. We found eager students everywhere wanting to get involved. We found professors who wanted to be engaged and connected. We didn't worry about the majority who did not want to move out of their comfort zone, but just concentrated on those who were willing. Sometimes, institutional engagement was weak, but we weren't seeking formal institutional support. We found more than enough interested students and faculty for our purposes. Other programs reported the same.

We found that it took a while for students to understand and accept new roles. Given a project in a community agency to help solve a problem, it took a couple of weeks for them to believe that no one already had the answer. Their experience of education was usually learning what someone else already knew and they just had to parrot it back to get a good grade. When they discovered that it was not an academic game and soon realized they knew more about their particular assignment than anyone in the world, they became excited and empowered.

In general we found it more effective to use a "project" rather than a "position" approach. The intern was given a manageable piece of research or task rather than being slotted into a job description. This suited the agencies better since "positions" were limited but potential "projects" abounded. Interns were like contracted "consultants" rather than "employees." Students enjoyed being active learners and contributors rather than simply recipients of learning or experience.

We found that agencies were eager to have able young men and women to help with some of the tasks they needed done. From a human resources perspective, students were a largely untapped resource for the newly recognized tasks of resource development and expanded community services. And they are located in accessible locations throughout the country.

In addition to the specific learning of an assignment—be it solid waste disposal, town renovation, legal services to the poor, employment opportunities, etc.—there were broader lessons to be learned that fit well into the goals of a liberal education at any level. Self-knowledge, problem solving, interpersonal relationships, organizational behavior, to mention a few, are skills and understanding that can be learned better in a service-learning setting than in the classroom or library. Providing opportunities for groups of interns to meet and share their experiences was important in expanding and deepening the learning dimension. They were asked to share not only what they had done but what they had learned. In this way they articulated their own learning experience and learned from each other.

One of the first interns was assigned to find out the circumstances of the closing of the public health clinic in a rural county of Tennessee that had no incorporated towns. He interviewed the medical personnel involved and reported back that they had to close because the county officials wouldn't agree to move from the current location, which they owned, to a more satisfactory facility. The young intern couldn't understand why county officials wouldn't cooperate to see that the people they were to serve had access to medical services. We asked if he had talked to the county officials. He indicated he hadn't and we suggested that as the next step. When he did so, he reported back that county officials said they were ready to improve the existing facilities, but the medical personnel wanted to move to a facility in which *they* had a financial interest. The real question was who was going to get the rent? He observed that it wasn't a case of good guys versus bad guys, but bad guys versus bad guys. That is a lesson we would do well to remember in this age of political polarization.

Another early intern, a young lady, was doing a living patterns survey of the population in a rural area. Interviewing a young man about area recreation opportunities she asked, "What is your favorite recreation?" Answers usually referred to hunting, fishing, bowling, movies, etc. Thinking to confuse the young lady he responded, "Sex!" She didn't bat an eye as she recorded his response and went on to the next question. "How far do you travel for this activity?" It was he who didn't know what to say, and she gained confidence and poise.

Another intern was exploring the possibility of establishing trash collection services and a landfill operation in a rural area of North Carolina that had no such service. A professor of political science was asked to be his university contact and learning facilitator. The professor complained that he knew nothing about trash collection or landfills but the technical advisor from TVA said the civil engineering questions were easy. "Tell me how many families will be involved and I can give you formulas that will tell how many cubic yards of trash will be generated, how many trucks will be needed weekly to move it, how big a landfill will be needed, what acreage is involved and the hours of bulldozer time required." The intern found the difficult questions were: Where would it be? Prevailing winds may play a role. Whose land was to be purchased or leased? Should the county buy trucks and hire drivers or contract collection to local truckers? How do you get people to cooperate by bagging up trash instead of dumping it in a ravine or along a roadside? Should it be paid for by a tax or a fee paid by the users? What relationship was possible with federal and state parks in the area? The political science professor, after helping the intern through the project and report, said the experience would change the way he taught his local government course to include much more about the real problems facing town and county officials beyond what state and federal laws say about municipalities.

The availability of students as a source of "manpower" for service was demonstrated dramatically in a project in Georgia. Georgia administrative districts had been asked to conduct a survey (I think it had to do with law enforcement) throughout the state. We were approached at SREB about finding students to do the surveys. We suggested that, in addition to the survey, each student be given a special individual task by the administrative district involved to help with a part of their development and community service activities. The districts liked the idea and we put together internships using our pattern and drawing on colleges and universities in all parts of the state. It worked beautifully. The survey got done and each district had helpful reports or services in matters of their selection. One student was to assist in a town restoration plan for a small town that had grown up along the railroad and parallel highway back in cotton production days. The town center was old and worn but still functioned with commerce for the surrounding area. The intern was an architecture student whose artistic eye saw some rather nice architecture on old buildings behind faded paint and dilapidated facades on Main Street. His report and drawings of how Main Street might look with removal of facades, minor repairs and remodeling, coordinated painting, traffic and parking modifications and landscaping, was a thing of practical beauty and much appreciated by the town. The student advanced his architectural education with excitement. And he got his part of the state-wide survey done.

The internship committee proved to be very useful in developing excellent student experiences, and high quality work and reports. It also engaged the agency, the college or university department represented and technical resources with each other through the intern. In many cases those relationships continued beyond the internship. There were cases of conflicting perceptions. An intern in western Tennessee was working on an employment/unemployment study which included identifying potential work force for industrial development efforts. The professor involved was not satisfied with a survey instrument that was being used and said he couldn't be associated with a project that was "faulty." The agency had employed a consulting firm to develop the survey and was satisfied that it would give them the information they needed for industrial development. The intern was caught in the middle and appealed to us for help. We were in no position to judge who was right but were clear about who was responsible. We encouraged the professor to make known his objections but then to defer to the agency, who had the responsibility. We suggested he discuss with the intern why someone would use a less than perfect survey instrument but that he not disengage himself, but rather be as helpful as he could. Fortunately he agreed.

In another case an agency official who had sponsored several interns observed that the program didn't need the universities' involvement. We persuaded him that it was important for the student and in the long run it would be beneficial to both agencies and educational institutions to work together seeking the best opportunities for service and learning for students. Students, trained at universities, will be the next generation of workers and teachers.

SOME OBSERVATIONS AND LESSONS

The hyphen in service-learning is important. It is meant to suggest a two way flow of communication. Service-learning is not simply applying what is learned in school to real situations but it links what is learned from experience to the learning of others which is taught in classes and read about in books. Service, without the learning element, can be narrow, rote, or otherwise limited. Learning without the service focus can be effete and self-serving. Keeping the two elements linked avoids the experience from being patronizing, self-righteous, or exploitive.

It is good for students to have opportunities to make contributions before they graduate from whatever level of education they are engaged in. The Danish philosopher, N. S. F. Grundtvig, observed that the purpose of childhood is not adulthood but childhood itself. This suggests that students are living now and not just preparing for life after graduation. And many of them want very much to be involved in the work of the world.

Learning is a lifelong process. It has been said that most educational dropouts occur at graduation. We reinforce a limited view of learning when we ask, "Where did you get your education?" Service-learning is a way to establish a pattern of learning from experience which will last a lifetime. In my Oak Ridge years I heard a lecture by Dr. Hubert Alyea, a Princeton professor of chemistry, which he entitled "The Lucky Accident and the Prepared

Mind." His thesis was that many important scientific discoveries were made when a "prepared mind" saw something that happened by accident and related it to other knowledge in a new way. He cited Newton seeing an apple fall and "discovering" gravity; Marie and Pierre Curie's discovery of radiation; a DuPont chemist, Roy Plunket, discovering "Teflon." None of these advances in science were the result of carefully designed experiments. Doesn't the same observation apply to other than scientific areas? Is our educational system preparing minds to see things in new ways? Approaching service with a learning link would seem to move in this direction.

Measuring learning is difficult. As questions of academic credit arose with interns, we quickly discovered how arbitrary most credit systems are. Credit assigned in the institution is largely a function of exposure hours. Credit for independent studies or field experience usually requires a report documenting what was done or observed. We didn't make any distinction between those situations where credit was a factor and where it wasn't. We expected the same quality of thinking and reporting in either case. The hard thing was to express what was learned. Interns were asked to go beyond telling what they did and to articulate what they learned. What do you know now that you didn't know before? What can you now do that you couldn't do before? What new questions do you have? Can you relate what you have learned to the insights of others expressed in books or lectures or sharing?

The issue of financial support was another complex question. Some felt that service had to be "volunteer" meaning unpaid. Some felt that getting both pay and credit was "being paid in two currencies." (An odious view of what credit should represent.) If academic credit is given it should be for the learning and not the service. We supported interns with a stipend or grant rather than "wages," although our view of service-learning didn't depend on financial questions. Is it less of a service if there is pay involved? Is there any difference in learning if pay is involved? We decided that financial support of whatever kind is a question of resources, context, circumstances, and motivation and could vary depending on the situation. Service-learning can be experienced in a variety of arrangements. Volunteerism is great but is not automatically service-learning. Being paid for services doesn't necessarily disqualify one from service-learning. Having no financial support may actually eliminate the possibility of participation by the lower income students who must show up at school the next term with a tuition payment not available from family. Peace Corps and other programs recognize this and provide support.

DEVELOPMENTS

As the variety of programs of service-learning grew and more agencies and institutions became involved, it was only natural that a desire to get together and explore this phenomenon arose. Two major national organizations were formed. The Society for Public Service Internships (I'm not sure of the exact title.) was led primarily by agency people and those of us who were involved in connections between institutions and agencies. The other national organization was the National Society for Experiential Education which was more institutionally based. It quickly became obvious that the two organizations had overlapping goals and membership. An agreement was reached to merge the two. The merged group became the National Society for Internships and Experiential Education. In my observation it has tended more in the institutional direction than in the agency direction. Perhaps this has resulted in educational values being more strongly represented than the "manpower" dimension.

Meanwhile back at SREB we were able to assist other regions in establishing their own service-learning internship programs. Since the SREB internships had grown beyond what could be well managed by a central program, we began to support decentralization. States began to set up their own programs. Some institutions started to feature service-learning programs of their own. Agencies developed their own relationships with universities. Service-learning was an idea whose time had come and the movement had a momentum of its own. Although the SREB Internships were still strong and would continue as part of the broader movement, I decided to start looking for next steps for myself. I was considering a position at the Department of Labor in Washington DC but got a call, out of the blue, from President Willis Weatherford at Berea College asking if I'd be interested in considering the position of Dean of Labor there. The result was that our family, with a new baby, moved to Berea, Kentucky, in the fall of 1970.

THE BEREA COLLEGE STUDENT LABOR PROGRAM

Berea College has a long tradition of serving able students, mostly from Southern Appalachia, who do not have the financial resources to pay for college. It has a strong commitment to the value of all people, taking its motto from the Bible: "God has made of one blood all peoples of the earth" (Acts 17:26, KJV). The community which gave rise to the college was anti-slavery and anti-sectarian, and Berea College was coeducational from the beginning. John G. Fee, the founder, a minister who was outspoken against slavery, was opposed to anything that separated people into classes. The Bereans were run out of Kentucky before the Civil War, but they returned, and the community and college grew as a monument to freedom. It was interracial until forbidden by Kentucky law from educating Blacks and Whites together, losing the court battle at the Supreme Court under the "separate but equal" doctrine. The student labor program at the college (and secondary school) was both a practical necessity and a philosophical statement. There wouldn't be those who work and those who don't need to. Everyone shared in the work that was needed. What an ideal setting for applying the principals of service-learning.

In the SREB service-learning internship programs, we had been dealing with a pretty select group of students and faculty. They were anxious to participate and highly motivated. At Berea all students were required to work regardless of their motivation. This raised questions. What is the difference between work and service? Is the working student a student or a worker? Are payments for student labor wages or financial aid? How are learning opportunities from labor experience maximized, realized and recognized?

Many students made good use of the opportunities afforded by their work assignments, but the general view was that it was a requirement and financial necessity. This became clear when I examined the patterns and found that most janitor jobs were filled by seniors. This was the easiest way to meet the requirement. Students are not dumb. A janitor could get 2 hours credit for cleaning an area that could be done in 45 minutes. I asked to see a list of students who were behind in their hours, thinking I'd call them in one by one to see what the problem was.

The list was over 300 names. Clearly, we had some work to do to make the program a vital, important part of the educational program for all students—not just the ones who had seen and taken advantage of the opportunities provided. The financial support was seen only as financial aid. Federal financial aid was in its beginning years and work-study payments were generally seen as the last resort, available when grants and loans still didn't meet full needs. Berea students received minimal funding from federal financial aid programs because Berea charged no tuition. Eligibility for aid was determined by considering room, board and incidentals only. Students who qualified for work-study funds were paid "extra" so two students doing the same job were getting different rates of "pay." The federal and state financial aid programs were designed for the very students Berea was serving, but because of Berea's "no-tuition" system this aid could not be claimed. Berea's financial aid budget was over $300,000 in the red as it tried to help students meet their needs beyond the tuition free provision. This was a problem that needed solving but also gave a tremendous opportunity to restructure the labor program and financial aid with new financial resources. The system was restructured over the next year or so and need not be recounted here except to note the changes that moved the labor program from just a requirement to being a part of the educational and student development offerings of the college.

How does one encourage service-learning in a student work program? Labor positions were reorganized into progressions reflecting growing experiences, greater service opportunities, and increasing learning expectations.

This was undergirded by a restructuring of financial support with payments increasing as the student rose in the progression. We began to talk of "labor as service to the community," the "labor curriculum" and "labor opportunities" instead of the "labor requirement." Some years later, I felt affirmed when one of our students who worked in a community outreach program was being quizzed by visitors. They acknowledged that he was doing community service but asked about the poor students who were doing janitorial work. The student replied, "You don't understand! The work of the student who is cleaning my residence hall is doing community service. If he didn't do his job, I couldn't do mine."

In his book *Working*, Studs Terkel reports a dismal picture of work in America, but also highlights "the happy few who find a savor in their daily job: the Indiana stonemason, who looks upon his work and sees that it is good; the Chicago piano tuner, who seeks and finds the sound that delights; the bookbinder, who saves a piece of history; the Brooklyn fireman, who saves a piece of life...." Terkel goes on to quote a waitress, whose "pride in her skills help her make it through the night." She says,

> When I put a plate down, you don't hear a sound. When I pick up a glass, I want it to be just right. When someone says, "How come you're just a waitress?" I say, "Don't you think you deserve being served by me?" (Terkel, S., 1972)

The processes of serving food are basically the same whether it is in the college food service, fancy restaurant, home, or soup kitchen. But it makes a world of difference to the one serving and the ones being served if it is done in a spirit of loving service. When work is done as a service both the work and the worker are transformed.

People often asked, "How do you motivate students to work?" I learned the answer from my SREB and Berea experiences. "Expectation!" To give a task, along with necessary resources, and expect him or her to complete it is saying: "You are needed! I believe in you!" This is motivating. On the other hand to say, "We will help you but we don't need you," diminishes self-worth. We never excused minimum effort by saying, "He's just a student," or, "Well, she is only a volunteer." We took a group of students who didn't fit well into regular assignments and made them into a team we called the ANTS (that stood for any non-technical service). There were lots of temporary jobs that didn't require highly developed skills, jobs which the plumbers, electricians, carpenters, secretaries, etc. would rather not have to do (like fix leaky faucets). ANTS could help with transportation to the airport, do inventories, prepare mailings, fix loose legs on chairs or set up for a meeting. We gave the ANTS training in all kinds of areas—driver training, CPR, minor plumbing and carpentry, special cleaning techniques, and anything that came along. Their motto was "We can do anything!" The supervisor of maintenance at the alumni building was their leader and he was a jack of all trades. The ANTS were called on for all kinds of tasks at no cost and minimum paperwork. They were very popular. This group of "misfits" became very productive and took great pride in their achievements. We called them the "swat team" of the labor program.

Once a new student came in to request an excuse from student labor due to a handicap she'd had all her life. Seeing her and knowing what a struggle she must have. I was emotionally ready to grant her request—but that was acting as if the student work was a requirement rather than an opportunity. So I declined the exemption and asked her to work with me to find some need that she could meet with the talents she had rather than focusing on the handicap. She became a valued member of the library staff. Everyone should have a chance to be productive.

DIMENSIONS OF STUDENT WORK
OR SERVICE EXPERIENCE

People tend to try to reduce things to one dimension, even though we don't really live that way. For example, when we buy a car we consider more than just transportation, or we'd all drive the same model. If we were primarily interested in safety we'd drive tanks. If we wanted speed we'd go for horsepower. If we wanted fuel economy we'd sacrifice space and power. If we wanted self-expression we might have opted for a convertible. We balance a variety of considerations as we do in most life decisions. Yet we sometimes pretend that we can only serve one goal at a time. A student work supervisor at the college press once asked me if he was supposed to get production out or train students. The answer, of course, is "Yes!" Student work or service experience is too often seen in only one dimension.

Financial

Working your way through college is an American value like apple pie. The financial considerations are important immediately, but are not the longest lasting value. Lessons learned from work long outlast the financial aid received at the time.

Doing a Job Well

Work has to be done to survive. Doing one's part is important and doing it well matters to oneself and to others. We depend on the steelworkers who make bridge girders for our very lives when we cross a river. The variety of tasks in an institution or community are all important to its well-being, and all can play a part.

Career Development

Clearly, there are advantages to choosing and furthering a career in work experience. What am I good at? What do I like? What do I dislike? Do I want to work with others or alone? In student work these can be explored in a safe environment. Many a would-be doctor or teacher discovers that career is not for them as a result of an internship or practice teaching. Others find their chosen field and get started while still a student. This is great on a resume.

Training

Much can be learned from student work. At Berea, students learn to weave, make furniture, cook, program computers, do library research, tutor others, and many other skills. The array of possibilities for learning is truly another curriculum from which students may choose. Some alumni report that little of the specific training they acquired as student worker applied to their later jobs, but assert that the lessons they learned in their work have been very important in their careers. One said, "I learned more about management in putting on plays as part of my labor assignment than I learned in graduate courses in management."

Education

One educational researcher when asked if student work could contribute to liberal education suggested that he didn't see how liberal education could be taught without it. Work experience can be a great teacher of basic liberal arts goals. Self-knowledge, interpersonal relationships, problem solving, understanding organizational behavior, self-discipline, critical thinking and other "virtues" are all potentially learned in the work experience.

Service

More than just doing a job, work is a contribution to community. It is an expression of self to something beyond oneself. The Shakers, a religious sect, were known for their simple living, beautiful furniture, crafts and creativity. They invented the washing machine and ice cream cone. They saw work as a form of worship. It was man's response to God and therefore must meet the highest standards. When work is performed in this attitude it is truly service and transforms the worker into something much more than slave or servant or just a wage earner.

Student work or service in a learning setting is multi-dimensional, offering a variety of benefits, which may change as time goes by.

SOME SUCCESSES AND DISAPPOINTMENTS

Obviously things don't go smoothly all the time. There are highs and lows. I had become Vice President for Labor and Student Life and we were successful for the most part in creating a service and learning environment for student work. We used the project approach wherever possible giving students opportunities to contribute something special beyond the daily routines. For example, one student responsible for scheduling use of rooms in the alumni building developed a guidebook based on her experience setting up for a great variety of gatherings. It showed different configurations for setting up tables and chairs depending on numbers and type of event. It was extremely helpful to users and staff as well.

Another example involved a student's summer job. "Sherry" was a premed biology major and an excellent student. Like all Berea students she had to earn some money during the summer and had worked the previous summer as a receptionist at the University of Kentucky medical research center. When I asked her about the coming summer she said they had invited her to come back. She said the work was boring but they paid pretty well. With her permission I called the director of the research center and identified myself. He confirmed that Sherry was going to work for them again and they thought very highly of her. I agreed that she was a very bright and lovely young lady and I asked if it would be possible to give her an opportunity to get involved in a piece of one of their research projects in addition to her receptionist duties. We discussed service-learning examples using a project approach. It would cost them no more and they might get more for their money. He liked the idea. The result was that Sherry operated on the eyes of salamanders under a microscope in a study of regeneration of tissue. She ended up with her name on a scientific publication reporting the results of the research. She also easily did her receptionist duties.

A less successful undertaking was again looking at summer work. I was aware that Berea students, and other low income students, could not afford to "volunteer" in community service in summers. They qualified for "work-study" support and most institutions used them for jobs on campus. I got in touch with Habitat for Humanity and got agreement that they could use interns with work-study support. They could provide for board and room at local sites with the help of supporters. Then I called 10 colleagues in various parts of the country whom I knew through the National Association for Student Employment Administrators and asked if they would be willing to set aside work-study funds for one or two students to work with Habitat during the summer. These directors of student work-study were all enthusiastic. Then I sent my assistant, Hazel Wehrle, to Atlanta to meet with federal regional officials responsible for work-study and make sure details were outlined for proper record keeping and reporting. Again, the response was positive and they agreed that the value of board and room could be used for matching requirements. I thought we had a good thing started, but then it fell apart. All the other colleges and universities bailed out. The work-study directors ran into negative responses from financial aid administrators, accountants, deans, and others who wanted to keep the funds on campus or didn't want the paper work hassle. Berea ended up sending two students who had a great experience but the vision of a countrywide way to give opportunities to low income students for summer service-learning internships disappeared. I suspect some creative college people have found ways to do this but I haven't heard of anything.

Another difficulty was experienced, this time with the federal bureaucracy. We were using the maximum work-study funds we could get and were able to get supplemental grants from funds turned in by schools that couldn't or didn't use their allocations. We received notice that under the "fair share formula" we were getting more than our share of work study funds and they would need to be reduced. That was the bad news, but they said the good news was that our students qualified for more grant funds and they could increase those. We pointed out that Berea chose to have a significant portion of financial support of students tied to their own efforts through the work program rather than depending only on the largesse of others, including the taxpayers through the federal government. After a considerable hassle we did get an administrative exception, but it showed the difference in priorities between those who see student work as a necessary evil when grants run out and those who see student work as an important opportunity for service and learning.

Unfortunately, some faculty members also have a negative view of student work, thinking it takes away from the academic program. To counter complaints that work interfered with academics we did a study of student achievements in both academic and labor programs. The only correlation between work hours and academic performance was at the extremes. Students who were failing academically had very poor work records. Students who excelled in academics worked the most hours and at the most responsible positions. A good student is a good student and a poor student is a poor student wherever they perform. Every year, the academic dean's list for the best students was also the list of the best performers in the work program.

A life-changing story of the impact of student work experience happened at Blackburn College which also has a required work program, although it does not serve exclusively low-income students. An international student from a well-to-do home was assigned to a work crew that cleaned bathrooms in the women's residence hall. She was horrified and found ways to stay on the fringes, trying to look like she was working. At home they had servants who did such things. In fact, they had servants who cooked, did the wash, made the beds and even laid out her clothes for her. After a time, she noticed that the other girls on the team were having fun. They talked and laughed as they worked and they discussed the best ways to make everything sparkle. They took pride in their work. She became interested and began to get involved, finding she also enjoyed a job well done and the benefits of working together. Learning about cleaning supplies and techniques was a whole new experience for her. When she went home for the summer she saw the servants in a new way. She talked to them about their work; she shared ideas about supplies and methods. Her family thought it peculiar but she had discovered a new dimension to life and a whole new set of friends. She went back to college and worked enthusiastically, eventually becoming the student manager of all the cleaning crews. She said it changed her life.

Blackburn, Berea, and other "work colleges" found a number of disconnections between the assumptions and requirements of federal financial aid programs and other areas of government regulation. I was given time off from my regular duties to work on these problems in cooperation with the other work colleges and eventually was successful in getting a provision in the Higher Education Act recognizing work colleges as a desirable approach to education and giving them special consideration.

SOME FINAL THOUGHTS

On a trip to Denmark, we were visiting different types of schools, one of which was what they call a "freeschool." Someone asked the principal of that school to define freeschool. He responded that to define freeschool would be to violate one of its principles. He went on to explain the movement as encompassing many varieties of educational approaches and configurations. I feel somewhat the same way about service-learning. We have a tendency to want to put everything in its proper box. When one is writing legislation or a program plan one must be definitive, but should not mistake that definition for the entire movement. Let service-learning be loosely defined as a linking of action and thought. Don't worry about whether it is high school or college, elementary grades or graduate studies. Let it be for pay or unpaid. Accept it with or without academic credit. Think of it more as a way of living and learning, than as an educational technique—though it is that as well. Dr. Margaret Mead, anthropologist, talked favorably about people with "leaky margins." These are people who are not bound by what is written but make their own notes in the margins. Service-learning has room for lots of leaky margins and this is good.

In spite of imprecise definition I would advocate service-learning as a very desirable form of education which can be designed appropriately for various educational settings, be it formal education or lifelong learning. A long-time friend and colleague, Bob Cornett advocates linking schools to communities as opposed to "top-down" education. He describes little Kingdom Come Elementary school in Line Fork, Kentucky as an example of community-based education. The school has adopted the project of restoring the American chestnut tree which was destroyed by blight in the first half of the 20th century. Shoots continue to come up from ancient roots only to succumb to the blight—but sooner or later, with help, the chestnut tree will come back. Citizens and foresters and community officials are all involved with the children. The fire department sponsors a chestnut fair each year. School is an exciting place to learn and to serve, as lessons are related to the school's passion for the chestnut tree. Kettering Foundation has published a little booklet with Bob's observations and ideas entitled, *Reclaiming Public Education.* Leaders of service-learning programs can give many examples of programs at all levels of education and can draw support and learn from each other without rote replication or cookie-cutter copies.

Service-learning has a values dimension deeper than being just another educational tool. Parker Palmer observed (if I can remember the wording), "Every epistemology has its own moral trajectory." My interpretation of this is that every way of knowing or learning has value implications. What values does service-learning promote? I have found those involved in service-learning are not self-seeking. They care for others and are willing to let others express themselves. They are not paternalistic but are eager to learn from those being served. They see students and "clients" as individuals each having worth. As in the story of the international student at Blackburn, learning in the context of service can enrich your life.

REFERENCES

Eberly, D. J. (1988). *National service: A promise to keep.* Rochester, NY: John Alden Books.

Terkel, S. (1972). *Working.* New York. NY: Pantheon Books.

CHAPTER 4

REFLECTIONS OF A MOBIOCENTRIC SERVICE-LEARNING PIONEER

Bob Sigmon

Bill Ramsay and Bob Sigmon began using the phrase Service-Learning in 1966 at Oak Ridge Associated Universities. Their pioneering 50 years ago and subsequent work in service-based experiential education motivated the editors to ask them to reflect on their experiences. These are Bob Sigmon's notes.

The 1960s were electric... the Vietnam War, student protests, Cold War, space exploration, racial tensions, voter rights and civil rights legislation, President Kennedy asking us what we could do for our country and the world, and the Peace Corps/Vista initiatives. Ellen Schall used the word "swamp" as a metaphor for these messy important public affairs concerns.

When Bill Ramsay and I were first operating a "Manpower for Development" internship program in 1966 we focused on three challenges: (a) In what ways can student manpower assist impoverished communities?; (b) How can we assist public and private educational and service providers in creating service-based experiential learning opportunities for young

Where's the Wisdom in Service-Learning?, pages 67–79
Copyright © 2017 by Information Age Publishing
All rights of reproduction in any form reserved.

people?; and (c) Can this work assist in preparing young people for roles in community development?

In the initial Manpower for Development programs we recognized the potential of community residents, community organizations, faculty, and students to expand their own imaginations and capacities for change in their situations. These observations suggested to us that "Manpower for Development" was too narrow a term and we found ourselves using "Service-Learning" to describe the mutual service and learning among the parties involved.

As we connected with Peace Corps, VISTA, City Corps, College Work Study staffs, college campuses and other local service-based learning activities we organized a Service-Learning Conference in Atlanta (1968), which became one of several initiatives that set in motion the creation of the National Society for Internships and Experiential Education (NSIEE) in 1972. By then, numerous governmental and higher education groups were promoting experiential learning connected to service or public oriented endeavors, each knowingly or unknowingly building on legacies of the Morrill Act, John Dewey, the Cooperative Education Movement, the WPA and CCC programs during the great depression, and returning Peace Corps volunteers.

Early on in service-based experiential learning programs I was reminded by a friend to look back and learn from examples of guild apprenticeships, church novitiates, ships' captain boys, job training programs today and listen to student protesters of the 1960s. She told me: "Real learning comes when interest is aroused by involvement... education, by definition, is the development of potential"... and then she asked, "is the leadership—business and governmental—willing to let some of their control rest in the hands of developing imaginations?" I kept these phrases before me on my bulletin boards for years.

Another significant counseling came from a Dean who warned me that promoting service-based learning practices in work places and educational centers would lead to a mobiocentric life pattern. That is, you will push the edge too hard and have to be mobile.

A campus based colleague and I had a conversation about our complementary roles in our work. He focused his energy on listening to students and finding ways to follow their instincts, offering support to find avenues for exploration and learning outside the academy. That is, he believed that "learning comes when interest is aroused by involvement." And then he observed that I tended to focus on systems—businesses, public agencies, non-profit groups, colleges and high schools, and communities—as being key players in "the development of potential" through promoting and engaging in service-learning activities for young people.

The early NSIEE conferences created space for conversations like these where a wide range of folks shared our gut instincts and challenged one another as we contributed to the growing capacity of institutions to engage cooperatively and faculty to open up to the potential for learning in situations outside the classroom.

For me, as the service-learning movement grew and matured, this mantra of "in the hands of developing imaginations" never left my consciousness as I became a mobiocentric campaigner for service-based experiential learning in the "swamp" in several settings.

However there were others who saw service-learning as "rocking the boat" and dangerous. The dean's insight about being mobiocentric became a reality for me. I was "let go" three times. Once in a state government role when a new party took over the governor's office. Then three years later by a university threatened by the success of a student initiated, community based program in a graduate school. I was told we had given too much attention to community based, student initiated learning and that did not square with the university function to pass on knowledge to students and the world. I was labeled as a "snake in the grass." And a third story was a mutual parting which placed me in early retirement.

PERSONAL STORIES AND REFLECTIONS

My first grade class in 1941 had 40 students. Our teacher was also the principal of the six room elementary school. When my buddy Sammy and I entered second grade, Miss Bell arranged for us to do our second grade work with her and also be tutors for her new first graders and be proctors for the class when she had to leave the classroom for administrative work. Looking back, years later, I could see seeds of service-based experiential learning being sown.

Leaving college I began a 3 year Methodist program for young adults and was assigned in 1958 to a rural village in Raiwind, Pakistan. The setting was a school for Muslim and Christian village boys and girls and a boarding arrangement for 12–16 year old Christian boys from surrounding villages.

The role assigned to me was boarding master for the 130 boys, which meant overseeing all their non-classroom activities. At the first Christmas season, two boys came to me with small presents. In my arrogance I said thank you but you need these things more than I do so please keep them. Bragging about this to a senior missionary several weeks later, she took hold of my collar and looked me in the eye, "You fool, you have denied those boys the joy of giving and showing their love for you. Until you can learn to be served by these boys you will be of no use here in Pakistan."

The notion of *serving and being served* by your actions and responses got hot iron branded in my spirit to go with "in the hands of developing imaginations." Another formative insight came from the many times young Pakistanis confronted me and showed me pictures of Negro citizens being hosed. "Go back to America," they said.

As I was concluding this work in Pakistan four issues were bothering me.

1. There had to be different ways to assist these children. Until the oppressive system is changed, these boys will have little chance for a productive future. Some begged me to help them come to America.
2. Looking back on that experience, it was a shock to realize that very little of my college education was of much utility in working with the boys.
3. In what ways could I spend the rest of my life in Asia promoting and encouraging the development of people seeking to come out of poverty? Where and how could I develop competencies for this work?
4. How was I to respond to the fellows challenging me to return to America to pay attention to the racial discrimination they were reading about?

Reflecting on these questions for 9 months in a seminary in Bangalore, India, some clarity emerged. I needed to live and work in the Southern United States to better understand its culture and history; I wanted to explore how to create opportunities for young people to serve and learn in challenging situations; and I wanted to reunite with a young woman I had met in Pakistan and see if she would marry me.

Returning to the states, I married the woman of my dreams and enrolled at Union Theological Seminary in New York City to focus on the concepts of service in the history of the Christian churches, learning about systems change strategies, and interning with a young adult program at Riverside Church working with young people from many parts of the globe.

In 1964, the American Friends Service Committee (AFSC) contracted with my wife and me for a two year assignment to develop a Southeastern USA program to replace their Voluntary International Service Assignments program that had to leave Haiti. The initial group of recent male and female college grads (men all conscientious objectors) also committed to a two year program. Each volunteer worked on tasks defined by the communities. In these settings, I became more aware of the teaching and learning reciprocity taking place between the young people and the community folk they were living and working among.

As the commitment with AFSC came to a close, my father was upset with me. Here I was a 31-year-old with a wife and child but never held a full-time job that paid a salary. He eased up when a real job emerged with Oak Ridge Associated Universities in 1966.

Working with Bill Ramsay at Oak Ridge Associated Universities allowed me to use my experiences growing up, in Pakistan, in New York City and the AFSC work to conceptualize internship models that focused on community defined needs, learning needs of students and faculty, and the potential of community organizations to be partners with the educators as service- learners.

By mid-1967, our program found itself in Atlanta at the Southern Regional Education Board and our staff of three now had a 15 southeastern state territory to promote service-learning practices. Mobiocentric again . . .

My work promoting service-learning was in North Carolina, South Carolina, Louisiana, Texas, and Virginia. With stipends available for students and faculty preceptors, we created opportunities in the 15 states for these service-based experiential programs to contribute to the wellbeing of many. Reflective opportunities were arranged in midsummer of groups of student service-learning interns to come together for a two day seminar. The seminars I facilitated focused on two issues: What are the major needs you see in your setting? And in what ways has your college education prepared you for addressing the problems? The intensity of the dialogue about education, jobs, discrimination, environmental issues, and other issues was alive and sparkling. Each intern was serving and learning at the same time. A consensus emerged that their college education was not helping them to understand and address the issues that were becoming important to them.

By 1969, the Governors of North Carolina (Robert Scott) and Georgia (Jimmy Carter) asked the Southern Regional Education Board to help create statewide programs in their state. I was invited to manage the North Carolina Internship Office (NCIO). A mobiocentric pattern continued into yet another swamp. The NCIO reported to the head of the Board of Higher Education and to the Governor's Chief of Administration, a major symbolic connection of the education and public service arenas.

With federal funds, limited state funds, and generous contributions from local communities and campuses around the state, NCIO had a 5 year run enabling 75% of the colleges in the state to initiate or expand service-learning activities. With a staff of outstanding students working part time and a secretary, we created and left a significant body of work in 5 years that set a stage for future programs.

In spring 1975, I left that job as a new political party wished me out of office and the university support saw us as "snakes in the grass." A book of stories of student service-learners entitled *Barefoot Learning in the Tar Hill State* (Willis & Wicker, 1973) was considered too radical for either of the sponsoring bodies to publish. The initial draft remains, unpublished, in a closet file in my apartment.

The mobiocentric pattern became real again as I joined the faculty of a new public health school at the University of South Carolina. The dean gave me a challenge. Take 20% of the curriculum and focus it on a student initiated and community based footing. I was now on the inside of the education system. Building on my prior experiences, a four semester sequence emerged with communities voicing their interests in sync with the graduate students' interests. As the third year of this work ended, the University leadership asked the dean and me to leave. We had, in their terms, given too much control for learning to the communities and the students and this was a threat to what the university stood for.

Fate responded again to the mobiocentric pattern. In 1978, I was back in North Carolina in a liaison role between Wake Medical Center and the University of North Carolina at Chapel Hill health science programs. The Wake Medical Center welcomed over a 100 students each day to serve and learn. Ten UNC-CH tenure track faculty were medical education teachers, researchers, and active medical care practitioners. Several of the continuing education and preceptor staff held faculty positions at UNC-CH. This model of a public service and learning was extraordinary. One of the many examples, private medical providers (at least 100 each year) provided preceptor assistance for the students as they cared for their patients. In the 13 years I served and learned there, I was convinced that here was a systems model that could work in county courthouses, city halls, nonprofit agencies, all sizes of businesses, state and national legislatures and staffs, and communities and their citizens banding together for this shared work and learning.

With the NSIEE staff located in Raleigh, I maintained an active and joyful working relationship with Jane Kendall and her staff and the work of the organization during this time.

Four defining service-learning formative statements emerged between 1979 and 1989 that grew out of the expanding creative efforts over the previous quarter century.

- Synergist (1979) commissioned me to write an article defining service-learning and these three points were highlighted.
  - Those being served control the service(s) provided.
  - Those being served become better able to serve and be served by their actions.
  - Those who serve are learners and have significant control over what is expected to be learned.
- In 1986 at an NSEE conference workshop, six practitioners expressed what their core values and practices were with respect to service-learning. A comment from a faculty member new to service-learning said,

> Now I see that the nuts and bolts are a means toward the end of experiential education...and that experiential education is a means toward the end of social action in the world....And social action is a means toward the end of what we are calling the Good.

- In 1987 the NSIEE (soon to be NSEE) agreed on its evolving mission statement:

  > As a community of individuals, institutions and organizations, NSIEE is committed to fostering the effective use of experience as an integral part of education, in order to empower learners and promote the common good.

- Three principles of service-learning were agreed on by the seasoned service-learning practitioners at a Wingspread gathering in 1989. Service-learning
  - allows for those with needs to define those needs;
  - engages people in responsible and challenging actions for the common good; and
  - articulates service and learning goals for everyone involved.

In 1999, Tim Stanton, Nadine Cruz, and Dwight Giles published *Service-Learning: A Movement's Pioneers Reflect on its Origins, Practice, and Future,* a thorough look at the movement.

With these evolving purpose and value statements and the wide ranging approaches to service-learning that were being practiced, I retired. Excited by the growth of programs, but disappointed that we were not doing well finding ways for the communities and those with needs being listened to and engaged as partners. The larger focus on student learning outcomes and curricular shifts were honorable, but in some ways a half a loaf in my pantry.

Summer 1991 found me hanging out a consultant shingle. I had sworn this would never be my lot, for my picture was that a consultant was someone who could not hold a real job. And yet it fit. I could not hold jobs, so why not become a consultant? My original expectation was to assist community groups, businesses, and governmental agencies explore and design ways they could be more proactive in listening to those they intended to serve and be more supportive of the young by designing service-based experiential learning in their settings. But very few requests came for this kind of effort.

So, I found myself designing and delivering dozens of servant-leadership workshops on the work and teaching of Robert Greenleaf. Greenleaf told me once that he felt providing services to those with needs in the traditional "recipient" modality was not useful. And went on to say that the real challenge is to wait for the those in need to claim and state their situation and then request what would be helpful to them, that is they would be "acquirers" of service.

Then, I began a ten year adventure with the Council of Independent Colleges (CIC) assisting in the design and implementation of four grant projects promoting service-based experiential learning for small private colleges and universities. Some of the creative work small colleges were doing with communities can be found in the *Journey to Service-Learning* (Sigmon, 1996), highlighting many of the voices of students and faculty, and demonstrating fresh patterns in the service-learning arenas. The book also contains my reflections and ruminations over a four decade service-learning landscape. A chart, "Organizational Journey to Service to Service Learning" from mid-19th century to the 1990s" is in this book. I hope someone(s) will fill it out more completely and bring it up to date soon, if indeed it has not already been done.

During the same period I worked part time with a leadership program in North Carolina designed to stimulate 30–45 year old promising leaders to develop their human relations understandings as they became leaders in the state. Service-learning guidelines for projects and servant-leadership themes were part of the seminar curriculum.

In 1999, my wife, our daughters and their husbands and I purchased a 14 acre farm Northeast of Asheville, North Carolina. Still working part time with these two projects, I became a market gardener, woodworker, handyman, beekeeper, sheep herder, and meddled some in community organizing in our community. Living communally with my grandchildren and children and their spouses was a wonderful way to grow old with some grace and joy.

By 2005, I had become more concerned about the earth. Thomas Berry and Wendell Berry became gurus for me. A mantra from T. Berry, "The earth is primary, humans are derivative," guides me to this day.

Elon University became interested in my files and papers. So the Elon University Archivist hauled off nine boxes of work notes, speeches, articles, research notes and collections of publications on service-learning which are now available from the Archives Department at Elon.

Giving up this collection was sad, for my inner self had wanted to take this history and produce a broader look than shared in this chapter. So I gave up that notion as Marian and I were preparing to leave the farm. Our daughters and their families stayed there. Marian and I began the challenges of a retirement village setting in late 2010 where I now produce practical wood implements from recycled wood and downed trees, try my hand at writing, do minor care of neighbor chores, and take vocal lessons.

Over the past couple of weeks drafting this piece, I have been reliving a fantastic adult life working in the service-based experiential learning arenas with a wonderful cast of friends in many places.

RUMINATIONS ABOUT REGRETS
OR MISSED OPPORTUNITIES

- I regret that in these early formulations of service-based experiential learning we did not pay attention to the earth and natural systems.

  > A unique experience had service-learning leap into my spirit several years ago. As a beekeeper, I went into a K–2 classroom with a bee hive (no bees). After showing the equipment and talking about the life of bees, we staged a simulation of an active bee hive. Who will be the Queen? Mrs. Anne, the teacher. Who will be the worker bees who have just been born? K students. Who will serve the Queen? First graders. Who will be the worker bees who go out to gather nectar and pollen? Second graders. Who will be the drones? Boys. (A drone's single purpose is to mate with the Queens.) Around the room were flowers, plants, apples, pears, and tree blossoms as sources for nectar and pollen. The room came alive with buzzing and movement back and forth to the hive and a range of activity within the hive. When the running around and noise was over, we chatted. I mentioned how impressed I was with how careful the older worker bees were when engaged with the younger bees…and how caring the new bees were of the Queen. We had sent the drones off to a far corner. Reflecting with these 5–7 year olds, I explained how the plants needed the pollinating role of the bees and the bees needed the nectar and pollen of the plants. I used the word "reciprocity." The teacher took over and wrote reciprocity on the board and interpreted it to the children. When that short exchange concluded, the children told me, "That is what we do all the time. We help one another out. We look out for one another." In the class was a blind girl, and I had teared up watching some of the girls gently assisting her during the exercise.

  Driving home in my truck with an empty beehive and the memory of those moments with these children, I saw a parallel that linked my life work finding creative ways for systems and individuals to serve and learn in mutually enhancing ways with what had just transpired in a K–2 classroom.
- I regret that early on researchers looked primarily at learning outcomes for students and encouraging faculty and curriculum changes. Very little was done to look at learning outcomes of faculty, of practitioners and the citizens with whom they worked.
- I regret not being more proactive in doing the research and sharing on how community institutions were adjusting to the potential of more and deeper service-based experiential learning.
- I regret that I did not work harder to urge more attention to the concerns and capacities of community practitioners.

- I regret that many of the early pioneers with social and community development experience became more and more marginal as faculty and curricular issues became the driving force.

WHAT IS ON THE AGENDA AS THE MOVEMENT EDGES FORWARD?

- In what ways will we explore how the earth and natural world of animals and plants are entwined with human life in service-learning work?
- How can more attention be focused on experimentation in workplaces and with local community groups and organizations as they become more attentive to teaching and learning? The Wake AHEC framework and others in the health sciences are worthy of closer looks. I often heard community organization folk say, "Involve us from the get go in designing, planning, implementation, and assessing of students who work with us." And another voice,

  > Healing the tensions experienced by community folk will occur when academic folk begin to let go of the need to be the expert and begin to realize that the community organizations are not passive recipients of outreach; rather they are active contributors to the teaching and learning process. Service does not flow one way.

  And "we urge campuses to invite more people to the table to evaluate an institution's role or project in a community."
- I long to see the day when citizens and institutions, service and educational, around the world encourage "developing imaginations" to work cooperatively using the basic principles of reciprocity, of mutual service and learning, and of movement toward just relationships as the bedrock of their evolving life patterns.
- I can envision requiring public service of all 18 to 20 year olds to work and learn while engaged in public service projects that promote skill and knowledge development along with promoting a sense of justice and peace with all participants? And linking unemployed men and women and underemployed folks in these service-based learning programs would be an exciting option. If those with greatest needs and young people together have a chance for such an opportunity, I believe we would see change that contributes to a more just society and reducing the income divide among us. I can envision foundations, local and state governments, religious groups, the policy makers with public education, higher education enterprises, 501c3 organizations, and thousands of small, medium and large business operations working cooperatively to sustain such a service-based experiential learning venture.

- But my most radical self wants to assert more strongly a notion I wrote about years ago asking us to "Sit down, Be Quiet, and Pay Attention." Not the way our teachers talked to us at one time, but the time is right for academic institutions and service organizations to slow down and focus on a thoughtful way, as Douglas Steere recommended, "to listen these communities into disclosure and discovery." That is, as communities figure out what they would want to happen and then engage the systems with whom they invite in to serve them well.
- As the service-learning phenomena grow and move on, it is my hope that the cooperative and supportive practice and spirit that kept so many of us engaged and encouraged will also be found in those engaging today and the near future in this essential work.
- In the CIC publication, *Journey to Service-Learning* (Sigmon, 1996), I shared a fable with this comment about results when communities work together with educators and students:

> Through the hands of developing imaginations, working in partnership with one another, these communities have created a framework for individual excellence to thrive, and for a variety of serving and learning opportunities for all citizens to grow. A literate, healthy, well-housed and expressive population with well-honed service and learning capacities will continue to focus regularly on the questions of "what is worth doing now?" and "what do we need to learn in order to do it well?"

ADDENDUM

There is a consistent theme in the places I was privileged to work where listening to and respecting community leaders and residents was consistently stressed and embodied in the work. But in many settings in my experience respecting and listening to community folk was not as intensive as I would have it be. But many of us early on sensed that if faculty did not get engaged, then the experiential learning in service type settings for students would not have a chance. So, we broker types were somewhat responsible for the imbalance. The page six purpose/goal statements over a 10 year span all highlight the community side of the work, but somehow in the 80s and 90s student learning outcomes, civic engagement, and striving to make experiential learning a part of secondary and post-secondary schooling dominated the field in my view. I have been absent from the main line literature for the past dozen years and perhaps the community voice has come back into the picture in a more equal way.

The main story line is that service-learning type work is an evolving, whirling thing. Ancient learning practices seemed to promote experience based learning as experienced folk created apprentice opportunities. This is still practiced, but in limited ways. John Dewey and others promoted experiential learning. I think the past 50 years some of us have tried to link the building up of communities with creative off campus learning/service work for students. And wanted to recognize the importance of the hyphen in the service-learning language. It seems to me the academy still has a significant way to go in reshaping the way students are expected to learn. When I was working the CIC, Rusty Garth and I argued for 10 years about this issue. He felt the colleges were just for education, not for community development. And I felt that the Whitehead notion of the "passing on the second hand knowledge" to the generations was maybe half a loaf. This pattern could be powerfully augmented in a fast changing technological world by engaging communities (residential, business, government, non-profits, et al.) in the creation of learning environments linked to community empowerment and challenge the issues of male domination, racism, and power in the hands of the money folk and systems as well as deal with the global warming crises and its implications.

When I was given the charge to create 20% of a new graduate school of public health, I was able for a few years to create a student initiated, community based possibility that could begin to address the issues in the previous sentence. But this higher education system was not ready for this, even in a small program. It was about this time that Ed O'Neill and others created a strong movement within the medical and health education world of linking learning and service . . . as had been shown in the university hospital setting in which I was privileged to work.

I will wrap this up by asking you and others a question. How long will it take for the academic leadership throughout our public and private systems to promote a practice whereby communities of many types are invited to the table to listen intently to communities and they, in turn, listen to the academy as both parties seek to offer creative and challenging environments for the young and not so young?

I think in the days of struggling in one and then another situation creating something new everywhere I went (I never had a job that had existed before it was given to me), my work and spirit was almost fully directed to the local setting. What I tried to do is share that with others in similar situations and we listened and questioned and learned from one another. The NSEE was a wonderful body for this sharing and learning. A "movement" was not on my radar screen during the intensity of the work in different places. So, responding to your inquiry in the words going before these may be nonsense to you and anyone else . . . Not sure this responds to your request for some more words, but this is what cometh forth on a rainy Tuesday afternoon in western N.C.

REFERENCES

Willis, J. and Wicker, R. (1973). *Barefoot learning in the tar hill state.* Unpublished manscript.

Sigmon, R. L. (1996, November). *Journey to service learning: Experiences from independent liberal arts colleges and universities.* Washington, DC: Council of Independent Colleges.

Stanton, T., Cruz, N., & Giles, D. (1999). *Service-learning: A movement's pioneers reflect on its origins, practice, and future.* San Francisco, CA: Jossey-Bass.

CHAPTER 5

HALF-FULL OR HALF-EMPTY ...WHO KNOWS?

Reflections on Forty-Five Years in Service Learning's Trenches

Timothy K. Stanton

AN ALIENATING EDUCATION

Pretty regularly in both professional and personal social situations I am asked, "How long have you been involved with service-learning?" My standard response: "Just about my whole adult life!" It's true. As a young high school student I followed political and social issues in the news. However, it didn't occur to me to engage with them directly until I found myself one Saturday marching down the center of one of Hartford, Connecticut's main streets in the middle of a fair housing civil rights demonstration. I was a senior and my English teacher had grabbed me and a couple of friends by the collar and taken us off to the march. I have no recollection of how that happened, but I can still see in my mind's eye the street and myself and my friends walking down the middle in a large, passionate crowd.

Where's the Wisdom in Service-Learning?, pages 81–92
Copyright © 2017 by Information Age Publishing
All rights of reproduction in any form reserved.

The impact was dramatic on all of us. We returned to school and immediately organized a civil rights club with the goal of raising the consciousness of our classmates about discrimination and civil rights issues and the fact that they existed not just in the South, but all around us in New England. Awakened in me was an urge to get involved, to meet and learn from new people outside my social circles, see new places and be a little part of history. That urge continues today.

The summer after I graduated I spent in Rockford, Illinois where I worked in an aircraft engine parts manufacturing plant. This experience was another eye-opener, this time into the issues of blue-collar factory workers and their labor relations. I became a member of the United Auto Workers and attended some of their meetings, spent time talking with the shop steward in our department, and tried through my chats with my co-workers to understand what was going on. My high school education, which carefully omitted labor history, had not prepared me well for these encounters.

This new awareness was the beginning of my alienation from my education. It seemed to me that the two most impactful educational events of my adolescence up to that point other than those related to peer relationships—the civil rights march and my UAW summer—occurred outside my schooling. I didn't know what that was all about then, but something was stirring. And that something was immediately strengthened in a number of ways when I arrived at Stanford University that fall of 1965. First, it was the dawn of the "late 60s" in Northern California. Civil rights debates and demonstrations were happening on and off campus that interested me. Provocative speakers, such as William Sloan Coffin, came to campus preaching support for the voting rights movement and resistance to the slow, at that time, build-up of U.S. troops in Vietnam, issues that spoke directly to my emerging, more conscious, political self.

I was smacked from the other direction in my freshman writing class. My instructor gave us a few free writing assignments during that first term and I chose to use them to reflect on the complex, troubling scene I had encountered in that aircraft engine factory. My instructor's response to these papers was horrible. I repressed most of his feedback long ago, but still remember the gold Phi Beta Kappa tie clip he wore on his narrow black tie every day in class. More importantly I recall my feelings at the time—ones of complete rejection—reading his scribbles all over what I thought was a thoughtful, critical and well-articulated paper and his summary response that the topic of my writing was not appropriate for "an academic essay." Thus, not only did I find my most learningful experiences to be outside my classrooms, I also found that when I attempted to connect them with my studies, my efforts were roundly put down. For me, this is where service-learning began. That freshman paper would be viewed now as a thoughtful analysis of deeply troubling reflections on a new, complicated, political experience. In those days, however, there was no academic space for such work.

I spent a good part of the rest of my four undergraduate years becoming involved pretty intensely in a volunteer tutoring program off campus, supporting and participating in anti-Vietnam War demonstrations on and off campus, and preparing for application for non-religious conscientious objector status from my draft board, which at the time had never approved one. Fortunately, I did find a few classes which supported these interests— English classes focused on the literature of the U.S. South and American history classes through which I could learn the history of poverty and discrimination that animated the civil rights work of the time; religion and philosophy classes that enabled me to discover and reflect on philosophical traditions—religious and secular—that animated my commitment to draft resistance. But, overall I gained my "higher education" on the streets of the campus, San Francisco and Berkeley, directly experiencing the tumult of the times, trying to be of service in modest ways, and participating in informal reflection sessions in the evenings with my similarly involved friends. These sessions were the "classes" that I most valued. Looking back they were service-learning.

ORGANIZING EDUCATION ALTERNATIVES

After knocking about for a couple of years post-graduation I landed a community youth organizing job at the Volunteer Bureau of Marin County. The savvy director at the time approached me at a community meeting, saying she had a donor who would support the organizing of a program to engage Marin high school and college students in community work. I took up the challenge and thought it would be easy. Go talk to the community non-profits and line up volunteer jobs for kids to do, go into the schools and recruit the kids and place them in these jobs. But quickly I ran into two serious problems: few non-profits were interested in having part-time, young volunteers around and those which did offered tedious, menial roles. Few students I encountered through my recruiting expressed any interest in taking these jobs. I had hit a roadblock. I quickly realized that the only way around it would be to organize projects that would involve young people in appealing, serious work that might actually make a difference in the community, and that meant starting from scratch. My associate and I spent the next few years organizing such projects. One was an alternative youth news-paper, which young people wrote for, edited, and published with the help of the county's weekly newspaper. Others were more politically designed to engage young people in the political process through events designed specifically for them. Bring the politicians to the youth rather than try to get young people to go to them.

Our most successful project involved organizing high school students to facilitate after school, therapeutic activity groups for middle school, "latch-key" children referred to us by mental health therapists. A social worker friend and I trained the students and they ran these groups. Two things happened fairly soon after we got started. The therapists began reporting that their young clients were getting better, their social skills were improving, etc., and they—the therapists—didn't think this was a result of the therapy. Something positive was happening in these groups. The high school students started to remark that they were learning more from their involvement in this program than they were in school. It was then that the light bulb went off in my head—What if this program was "school?" Perhaps projects like this were ways to connect and integrate two realms that were mostly disconnected—one where people thought a lot and never did much with it (the academy) and the other where people were very active working to try to improve the world, but never thought much about their actions or linked their thinking with relevant knowledge of what is already known.

With these thoughts dancing in my head I came across an announcement for a conference in Los Angeles organized by the Society for Field Experience Education. Publicity lead me to believe that I might find there other people doing work similar to mine, with whom it would be good and helpful to interact. So, off I went to Los Angeles, little knowing that at this meeting I would meet a number of individuals doing fascinating work, many of whom would become long-term professional colleagues, collaborators and friends. I would find a home for what seemed to be my calling. The rest of my professional life was about to unfold.

A LIFE OF SERVICE-LEARNING

Some of that life looks like this. I had 7 years at Cornell University directing what was called the Human Ecology Field Study Office, which sponsored New York City-based and Ithaca-area field studies, which were clearly service-learning. Three incredibly gifted colleagues and I developed that little program into an exemplary, path breaking one with a national reputation for excellence in our then nascent field. All four of us were called upon to write and speak about our work at conferences and workshops around the country. However, when we returned to Cornell, most faculty colleagues treated us and our program, though loved by students, with scorn.

We had at least several things going against us regardless of what we felt was very high quality educational and community development practice. One was that it was experiential learning—a no-no at the time in higher education. Our faculty colleagues thought we were putting students in situations out of our and their control. Where was the subject matter, they asked? In addition, our curriculum was interdisciplinary, also work not highly esteemed in an academy dominated by faculty members rooted to their disciplines. It didn't fit anywhere that our colleagues could or would understand. Another challenge was that as an interdisciplinary, extra-departmental program none of us held regular faculty posts and only one of us had the standard academic qualification for having such a post—a doctoral degree. So, we were suspect on that most basic level. After 5 or 6 years of struggle to maintain our program and budget, it all began to unravel. Soon I found myself back in the Bay Area more alienated from formal, higher education than I was when I graduated.

GAINING SOME WISDOM

I gained wisdom during these difficult, but very exciting early years. With my Cornell colleagues I learned how to carefully design my service-learning courses as structures that enabled students to develop a discipline of clear perception of their experiences, the people and issues they confronted, and of the impact, or lack thereof, of their efforts to be of service. I learned to lead them through reflective processes designed to unpack the concept of service itself. I learned to enable them to become empowered, confident, self-directed learners capable of setting their learning and serving goals, and independently working toward them and assessing their progress. Equally important to me, I learned how to build a community of service-learners committed to assisting each other in both their service and learning.

My Cornell colleagues and I all came of age during the late 60s. We all shared frustrations with conventional pedagogies and their passive, uncritical approach to knowledge assimilation, and we became closely bonded. We bonded as well due to the fact that we had to "circle our wagons" and protect ourselves against the ongoing onslaught from the wider institutional environment. Our friendship was our defense. These bonds gave us strength. Nevertheless, it was still lonely work as collegial relationships beyond the walls of our offices and the students and community partners we worked with were hard to establish and sustain.

The saving grace for us and for so many of our like-minded colleagues at other institutions at the time was the Society for Field Experience Education, which later evolved into the National Society for Internships and Experiential Education (NSIEE). Its annual meetings were support group sessions in many ways. Not only did we share our work, as many other professionals do in their associations, we engaged in deep dialogue in sessions and at the hotel bar about who we were and what we were about. We shared and helped solve each other's problems and challenges. We debated the assets and liabilities of our marginal positions within the academy. Gradually we began to write for NSIEE's newsletters and books, and other outlets. Jane Kendall, NSIEE's excellent director and shepherd of this movement, encouraged this work and developed a number of us into an amazing consulting corps able to bring service-learning to institutions just beginning to consider it. Reflecting on my experiences with this widespread community of friends and colleagues, I came to perceive the need and importance to change agents of having a support network outside of the challenging environments in which we worked. We needed each other, because we had so few like-minded souls to relate to on each of our campuses. We couldn't have accomplished what we did without the network, without each other. My experiences of conferences of Campus Compact, IARSLCE, and other groups these days is similar. We need these networks as much as they need us.

MOVING BACK TO STANFORD

In 1983, Stanford called. President Don Kennedy had inaugurated what became known as the public service initiative, with a goal of encouraging and involving undergraduate students to get involved in volunteer service—through local community organizations, government, and any other way. His belief was that young people privileged to attend a place like Stanford had a special obligation to engage in public service, and that an institution like Stanford had an obligation to encourage and support them in doing so. I read about this while still at Cornell and wrote to Kennedy, praising his initiative, but asking why this obligation to be civically engaged rested solely on students? I was not in the habit of writing to university presidents. Indeed, this was the first such letter I wrote, but I found Kennedy's "op-ed style" essay in the alumni magazine to be the first thing I had seen from Stanford that made me proud to be an alumnus.

So, I wrote Kennedy praising his initiative but also asking why there was no evident aspect of it that connected the effort with Stanford's core academic mission. Shouldn't this initiative, I asked, be explicitly connected to that mission? Shouldn't faculty also become more engaged with communities off campus—not as volunteers necessarily, but through their scholarship and through providing spaces in the curriculum for students to reflect critically on their community experiences to ensure that they were educational, that this learning was integrated with their studies and reason for being at Stanford, and to help ensure that their service was positively impactful or at least did no harm? Kennedy responded positively to my letter, which led me to begin visiting the Stanford campus and participate in discussions about the new initiative in 1984–85, when I had returned to the Bay Area on a leave year from Cornell.

As a result of these visits I was invited to write a job description for the first full-time position at a new center for public service, which Kennedy and colleagues wanted to establish, and apply for the job. I spent the next 15 years helping to establish the Haas Center for Public Service and build service-learning into and across Stanford's curriculum. I assisted Kennedy and others in establishing Campus Compact, and laying the foundation of its work to embed service-learning into the curricula of its member institutions and give birth to what is now known as the wider movement for civic or community engagement.

In those years, as well as at Cornell, I was greatly assisted by my encounter with David Kolb's theory of experiential learning, his "experiential learning cycle" (Kolb, 1984). I first met Kolb at an NSIEE conference in Washington, DC in 1978 where he was a keynote speaker. He described his research that resulted in his theory development and the "learning cycle" diagram. At this conference, and subsequent ones, we talked about Kolb's work and debated how true to life we thought it was. John Duley, one of service-learning's earliest pioneers based at Michigan State University and mentor to many of us younger ones, was perhaps most critical. He thought that Kolb's theory, with it's one dimensional, one directional, staged sequence leading from concrete experience through reflection, abstract analysis and active experimentation, to be much too simple to describe the complex process of human learning. He advocated a "basketball theory" with numerous relationships among and along Kolb's stages and axes.

I found these debates very stimulating and enriching in an academic sense. However, I was more taken by how Kolb's model, whether "true" or not, presented practitioners with a marvelously helpful framework on which to design and hang their work. This was because it demands that we think through in most concrete ways:

- what and where students' service experiences will be and how, when, and by whom they will be structured, supported, and assessed;
- what students will be asked to reflect on as part of their service-learning, who will facilitate that reflection, how, where, and when;
- how these reflections will be connected and integrated with related theoretical knowledge by whom, how, where, and when; and
- how, when, and with what facilitation the new theories students induce from this staged, integrative, critical reflection process can be tested out in their ongoing experience.

In other words Kolb's model gave me a check-list of everything I needed to consider, plan for and do to make my service-learning courses a high quality experience for my students and helpful and useful for my community partners. As importantly, it gave me a way to speak with faculty colleagues at Stanford about how service-learning could become a knowledge development process for students that could be structured and assessed in not too dissimilar ways from conventional teaching and learning. In other words, by stressing the knowledge development possibilities and outcomes of service-learning and their relationship to departmental academic curricula, I could help faculty members see how service-learning could take its place as a respected, widely used pedagogy at Stanford. I have used Kolb's model in similar ways in my consulting work with faculty and administrators across the United States and overseas, continuing to refine it as a check-list for curriculum planning.

I stepped down from the directorship of the Haas Center in 1999 and spent the early years of this century helping to establish and direct a concentration in Stanford's Medical School on community health and public service. I never once thought I would spend a minute in a medical school. However, a group of medical students there in 1999, including some who had been Stanford undergraduates and what we called "Haas Center groupies," had written a manifesto-like position paper addressed to the school's deans. It described how lacking their medical education was in opportunities for teaching and learning about communities and about how physicians could address health challenges at the community level, which was where they understood these challenges would need to be addressed, rather than through seeing individual patients in the doctor's office. I found their paper, like Kennedy's earlier one, to be extremely compelling, and so had the deans. They allocated funds for a community health curriculum and told the students to find a director to help establish it. They found me. Thus, we embarked on a new program, which included a core service-learning seminar for first-year medical students and a year-long community research program. This little program soon became one of several "concentrations" in the MD education curriculum. By the time I left, the admissions office was highlighting the concentration as a draw for students of color. Surprisingly, but pleasing to me, it was the concentration with the most enrolled students.

I mention this aspect of my work experience not just because it marks my first foray into building service-learning into graduate level education, an early such effort in graduate education, more generally. I do so, as well, to share two additional points. One is the importance of students in building this movement. The medical school concentration never would have occurred if it wasn't for this small group of hugely dedicated, and exceptionally thoughtful and articulate students, who persuaded the school to shift its priorities. Students played a similar role in the establishment and building of the Haas Center. Don Kennedy often talked about how his interest in promoting public service was greatly stimulated by students who knocked on his door in the early 80s saying not all of them wished to head to Wall Street. Some were engaged or wished to engage in community service and development and they asked: What was Stanford going to do to support them and encourage others to take a similar course? In our early days at the new center it was students' widespread and enthusiastic response to Kennedy's call to service that energized our work, and often led us to develop programs, some of which have continued some 25 years to this day. Looking across our field and its history, including the work of Wayne Meisel and Bobby Hackett and COOL (Campus Outreach and Opportunity League), one must conclude that students during this era were as important in bringing about social and institutional change as our generation had been in the 1960s.

A second point was my experiencing once again the importance of national, collegial networks and associations from which to gain encouragement, support and opportunities to learn and interact with colleagues. During this time, the two networks I interacted with most were Community-Campus Partnerships for Health, which has developed itself into a comprehensive resource for practitioners in health fields to learn about and share wisdom related to service-learning and community-based research. The other was California Campus Compact. Its excellent director, Elaine Ikeda, invited me to head-up an initiative on community engagement and graduate education, which took me around the state leading workshops and introduced me to a most wonderful group of energized, hungry for service-learning graduate students just getting started at building this work into graduate schools in the humanities and professional fields.

During my last decade at Stanford, I established and directed an Overseas Studies Program in Cape Town, South Africa, which focused on service-learning and research with Western Cape NGO partners (McMillan & Stanton, 2014). This wonderful and challenging work built upon knowledge and contacts I had made through a 7-year consulting relationship with Community-Higher Education Service Partnerships, which took me across South Africa working with faculty, students, and community members seeking to build partnerships through which the country's higher education sector could contribute to building the "new South Africa." Observing and participating in a rapidly developing community engagement field there presented me with many opportunities to reflect on how our work develops differently in varied geographical regions and cultures (Stanton & Erasmus, 2013; Xing & Ma, 2010). I have been fortunate and privileged to have similar experiences working to develop service-learning with colleagues in Southeast Asia. However we conceive of it, we are part of a worldwide phenomenon, which will benefit from comparative analysis.

LOOKING FOR WISDOM

These wonderful and sometimes very hard years have enabled me to do much reflection on and theorizing about the development of our field. On a given day I can feel that we have accomplished much, that higher education has truly changed to enable me and so many colleagues to practice this work in a safe and encouraging environment—so different from those early years I had at Cornell. However, on other days, and in reflection with colleagues who entered the field around the same time as me, I wonder how has this happened? Has higher education really changed all that much? Or, has our work, which had actually been dangerous for many in the early days, lost a bit of its edge as we, myself very much included, worked to institutionalize it in academic departments and disciplines (Stanton, 1998). I am not sure, but I continue to have this parallax view of our accomplishments.

On the one hand, certainly we've come a great, long way. In the early days simply surviving in our jobs and building a practice was a major achievement, and many bodies were left along that road.[1] Since 1985, as well documented by Hartley and Saltmarsh (2016), with the establishment of the Compact and later the federal government's Corporation for National Service Learn and Serve program, service-learning has proliferated across higher and secondary education in the United States and in this century around the world.[2] Who can complain about this?

Yet, on the other hand, what exactly is it that has been embedded within the academy and somewhat institutionalized? Has service-learning lost a critical edge along the way as a much broader, and in some minds fuzzier, concept of community engagement replaced it? Thirty years after 1985 many colleagues are beginning to ask such questions, many of which concern the degree to which the "pedagogification" (Pollack, 2015) of service-learning in disciplines and departments has weakened its interdisciplinary embrace of an "undisciplined real world." This process favors the academy's value of student development over community development goals. Another set of questions arises with a sense some have that current practitioners and scholars concerned with this work see themselves more as taking steps on a career ladder developing in higher education, rather than as institutional community organizers and change agents sitting in institutional margins with feet in both campuses and communities, which is how many of the field's so-called early pioneers viewed themselves.[3] Is an important, critical perspective on both the institution and community lost when one moves from the margin to the mainstream of an institution?

An additional area of concern for me is the evolving practice itself. For example, in our proselytizing with faculty and other institutional colleagues, and in our literature, we call for and celebrate the importance of critical reflection on service experience as a hallmark of good practice.

But just what do we mean by critical reflection specifically? What does it look and sound like? What kinds of reflection prompts are likely to lead service-learning students to deep, critical questioning of their experience and of themselves in it, to perceive all of this more clearly than they otherwise might? Or, what kinds of changes are we seeking to bring about with our community partners? What are the specific, concrete roles of students and campus-based practitioners in this work? In my travels I don't come across much deep deliberation on these kinds of what I call "what do I do on Monday" questions, and it worries me. Having built a field that is publicly supported by both college presidents and even some politicians, have we become complacent and lost some of our commitment to developing "critical consciousness" (Freire, 1970, 1973) in students, community and institutional change, social justice? I don't know for sure, as my circles are admittedly limited. However, I hope this brief ramble spurs us toward a more critical stance toward our most critical work.

NOTES

1. See Stanton, Giles, and Cruz (1999) for detailed accounts of these perceptions by service-learning pioneers.
2. For examples, see Talloires Network at: http://talloiresnetwork.tufts.edu
3. See Stanton, Giles, and Cruz (1999) for detailed accounts of these perceptions by service-learning pioneers.

REFERENCES

Freire, P. (1970). *Pedagogy of the oppressed.* New York, NY: Continuum.

Freire, P. (1973). *Education for critical consciousness.* New York, NY: Seabury Press.

Hartley, M., & Saltmarsh, J. (2016). A brief history of a movement: Civic engagement and American higher education. In M. Post, E. Ward, N. Longo, & J. Saltmarsh (Eds.), *Publicly engaged scholars: Next generation engagement and the future of higher education* (pp. 34–60). Sterling, VA: Stylus.

Kolb, D. A. (1984). *Experiential learning: Experience as the source of learning and development.* Englewood Cliffs, NJ: Prentice-Hall.

McMillan, J., & Stanton, T. K. (2014). "Learning service" in international contexts: Partnership-based service-learning and research in Cape Town, South Africa. *Michigan Journal for Community Service Learning, 21*(1), 64–78.

Pollack, S. S. (2015). Critical civic literacy as an essential component of the undergraduate curriculum. In W. J. Jacob, S. E. Sutin, J. C., Weidman, & J. L. Yeager (Eds.), *Community engagement in higher education: Policy reforms and practice* (pp. 159–181). Rotterdam, The Netherlands: Sense.

Stanton, T. (1998). Institutionalizing service-learning within postsecondary education: Transformation or social adaptation? *Partnership Perspectives, 1*(1), 9–18.

Stanton, T. K, Giles, D. E., & Cruz, N. I. (1999). *Service-learning: A movement's pioneers reflect on its origins, practice, and future.* San Francisco, CA: Jossey-Bass.

Stanton, T. K., & Erasmus, M. A. (2013). Inside out outside in: A comparative analysis of service-learning's development in the United States and South Africa. *Journal of Higher Education Outreach and Engagement, 17*(1), 61–94.

Xing, J., & Ma, C. H. K. (2010). *Service-learning in Asia: Curricular models and practices.* Hong Kong, China: Hong Kong University Press.

CHAPTER 6

THE WISDOM
OF JANE SZUTU PERMAUL

Jane Szutu Permaul

Where's the wisdom in service-learning? Even though service-learning has been a part of my life, I have not reflected on it for many years, having enjoyed a satisfying career involving service-learning one way or another for over 40 years, the last of which was the design and the implementation of the W. T. Chan Fellowship Program in 2001, a cross-cultural service-learning program where I pretty much had the freedom to apply all the good principles and practices of service-learning (2010 and www.lingnanfoundation.org). So, with time away from "direct involvement," I may learn something about service-learning which was not possible when one is focused on particular demands and challenges.

The notion of service-learning preceded its name and language. Among the many notable quotes by Confucius (551–479 B.C.) stated, "I hear and I forget. I see and I remember. I do and I understand." And another quote stated, "By three methods we may learn wisdom: First, by reflection, which is the noblest; second, by imitation, which is easiest, and third by experience, which is the bitterest" (Confucius quotes; Google search). And from the west, Aristotle stated, "For the things we have to learn before we can do them, we learn by doing them" (*Nicomachean Ethics*, Bool II, page 1).

Where's the Wisdom in Service-Learning?, pages 93–99
Copyright © 2017 by Information Age Publishing
All rights of reproduction in any form reserved.
93

John Keats (1795–1821) in *The Letters of John Keats* wrote, "Nothing ever becomes real till it is experienced. Even a proverb is no proverb to you till your life has illustrated it" (Forman, 1895/2011).

The more contemporary notion of service-learning and the actual adoption of the term, came in the early 1970s emerging from the National Society for Internships and Experiential Education founded in 1971, through which many of us who worked separately scattered across the country came together, finding common ground, and decided that we can benefit from mutual support and have much to learn from each other. The National Society for Internships and Experiential Education is a "society" and in many respects represented more than any one profession. Our common ground was learning from various experiences. Service-learning added another dimension of serving, which we found provided additional learning to those who engaged in it.

INITIATE AND PURSUE OPPORTUNITIES

I fell into service-learning in 1973, when the notion of service-learning was just emerging. Prior to that, I was involved in developing experiential education in response to undergraduates' inability to find meaningful employment, caught in the revolving door of having to have experience before being employed and not able to get experience without employment. That is when cooperative education and internship came into being and many of us simply broadened those efforts to experiential education. Service-learning provided learners and the communities more value than just an experience. Whereas cooperative education and internship were more career-oriented for undergraduate students, service-learning was more oriented to liberal educational goals of communication, inter-personal relations, humanities, social dynamics, civic engagement, and public policies

The first opportunity for me came toward the end of the Vietnam War, as it dragged on (1964–1975). More and more veterans returning home needed assistance to reintegrate into American communities. The late Senator Alan Cranston from California was actively engaged in finding adequate support for these veterans, while Governor Ronald Raegan was determined to close down most residential mental facilities in California. Veterans were driven into "group homes" provided by landlords more interested in the rent receipts than the reintegration of veterans to their home communities. Fortunately, the University Year for Action, "a federally funded program that let students work firsthand with some of the problems of our society; drug abuse, poverty, the elderly, and the mentally ill" (1972) was established by the Nixon Administration. Given the challenges at that time, the University of California, Los Angeles (UCLA) became the beneficiary of a multi-year grant which mobilized its students to work with veterans residing in group homes scattered in greater Los Angeles. Students assisted veterans with basic every day skills, such as shopping for food, clothing, toiletries, and other personal items. It was an amazing experience for our students, with many seldom bothering with such activities. The students transported selected group activities from campus to the group homes, enabling the veterans to both enjoy each other and engage in their home communities. Students built relationships with veterans and learned about many matters they may have otherwise taken for granted. Most importantly, they learned about various aspects of mental health and what responses were needed to either support veterans or help them to heal and rebuild their mental capacity, not to mention dealing with the impact of war. That was my first experience in service-learning, although I did not know that was what it was called.

The University Year for ACTION was one of many programs under the ACTION federal agency, created by president Richard Nixon, to promote volunteerism among citizens to help others (to include established programs, such as VISTA). Subsequently, each U.S. president created variations to promote volunteerism. President Bill Clinton finally merged all federal programs under one federal umbrella in 1993 and created the Corporation for National and Community Service. These federal supports gave birth to service-learning on many college and university campuses, with more stress on volunteerism and civic engagement than learning from it. The Corporation changed form and emphasis with each change in the White House. But UCLA, to this day, still takes advantage of federal support to involve undergraduates in service-learning.

To access federal support for service-learning, stressing both the service and the learning, one had to go to more traditional sources, such as the Fund for the Improvement of Post-Secondary Education and one of the national institutes. These were traditional agencies, and difficult to infiltrate. One highlight was getting a grant from the National Endowment for the Humanities on a project, Applied Humanities and Chicano Studies, partnering with a prominent History and Chicano Studies professor at UCLA (1981–83). That project opened both the History and the Chicano Studies at UCLA to engage their students in service-learning beyond the project. We actually participated in a panel discussion on "Applied Programs and Internships: Student Perspectives" at the National Council on Public History Annual Conference, April 1985 in Phoenix Arizona.

In 1985, presidents from Brown, Georgetown, and Stanford Universities founded the Campus Compact, a coalition of college and university presidents to counter the "me generation" image of their students by engaging students in community service. This coalition today involves about one-third of all colleges and universities nationally and expanded the efforts not only with presidents, but faculty, staff and students, as well. In 1991, the Campus Compact created the Integrating Service with Academic Study initiative. Many of us were both advocates for developing such an initiative and took advantage of it in developing service-learning in our respective campuses. We also encouraged our respective presidents to get involved, hence beginning to receive support from the very top of colleges and universities. In 1990, California, under the leadership of President Donald Kennedy from Stanford and Chancellor Charles Young of UCLA, created the California Campus Compact, which brought resources closer to those of us in California. The Compact's work as an independent agency propelled service-learning forward, especially at the higher education level. But, because so many of the service-learning projects were partnerships between college-university with K–12 education, service-learning spilled over to K–12 world, as well.

Once again, service-learning had been practiced in isolation by individual teachers at the secondary education level, before they discovered that there was a name for such teaching-learning practice. Once discovered, with teachers using service-learning to reach out to each other, service-learning began to flourish at the middle and high school levels.

Having reached institutionalization of service-learning in many colleges and universities, international students returning to their homeland, especially to Asia and Pacific Islands, began to introduce service-learning to their faculty and fellow students. With the sustained support from two private foundations from the United States, Lingnan Foundation and United Board, both dedicated to South China higher education, service-learning was introduced in Hong Kong, first at the Lingnan University, Hong Kong (LUHK) in 2005. Many Pacific Island universities, especially those founded with a religious base, began to adopt service-learning as part of their devotion to serve the needy. Fu Jen University of Taiwan was among the leading universities to adopt it. By 2007, the first Asia-Pacific Islands Regional Service-Learning Conference took place in Hong Kong. People's Republic of China had no representative at the first conference. Again, LUHK reached out in their exchange program with Chinese universities and, by 2010, China was beginning to engage.

The Hong Kong University Grants Commission (the equivalent to the state funding agencies for public universities in the United States) encouraged service-learning in Hong Kong by providing a special grant program for campuses in the development of service-learning program. And, as the Hong Kong government moved from a 3 to 4-year bachelor degree program, many of the universities added service-learning in one form or another to the graduation requirement, where most were in the format of academic offerings. On the Pacific Islands, most of the service-learning programs, while inspired by religious-based universities, were programs dealing with student development and social issues, such as those found at Fu Jen University in Taiwan.

Once again, the movement of service-learning to Asia and the Pacific Islands was not by accident. It was introduced by people who were inspired and took their service-learning back to their respective homeland.

RESEARCH, EVALUATION, AND DEVELOPMENT

Most of our experiences in advocating and developing service-learning programs and opportunities had been successful. About 30% of U.S. colleges and universities have opportunities for their undergraduates, as reflected by the active membership in Campus Compact. Sadly, few schools or departments of education have embraced the study and research on service-learning. Education faculty seemed to limit their studies to passive versus active learning.

On the other hand, instructional evaluation of service-learning offerings on colleges and universities were pervasive. These evaluations yielded positive findings and propelled the growth of experiential education and service-learning on college and university campuses. Does service-learning really produce learning? What kinds of learning? Do service recipients really receive meaningful and intended service? How do you know, from program to program, that they are fulfilling the goals of service and learning? How do you evaluate a program and document its impact? Is it worth academic credit? If so, what should be the standards in granting academic credits? The questions were endless, and frankly continued at many colleges and universities and secondary education.

These evaluations led to the curiosity of some faculty, primarily from the social sciences and developmental psychology, and eventually to the beginning of independent research on service-learning. These researchers helped to identify what service-learning generated among those who engage in it, be they students, facilitators-faculty, service recipients, community partners, or educational institutions. Most findings had been positive. Findings that were questionable or outright negative helped to refine and the strengthen program design and practices. The American Association for Higher Education (AAHE, now AAHEA, with the additional "A" standing for "Accreditation"), developed a series of papers on service-learning. An excellent article, "Models of Good Practice for Service-Learning Programs" by Mary Kay Schneider (Schneider, 1998), was a good example of the value of this new independent research.

The National Society for Internship and Experiential Education and Campus Compact also supported research and publications on service-learning. Further, as a result of research findings, we found new forms of service-learning to accommodate various learners with different learning styles, as well as the needs of community partners. A review of various forms of service-learning practiced today have been categorized, based on identification of service-learning projects by Cathryn Berger Kay (2010) and summarized by Carol Ma and Alfred Chan at the Office of Service-Learning at LUHK, to include:

- Direct service-learning in which students served individuals in need directly and learn from the experience;
- Indirect service-learning in which students worked on broader social issues which benefit the local and broader community, such as environmental projects;
- Research-based service-learning, in which students gathered and presented information on areas requiring further knowledge needed for resolving community or social issues or servicing needy individuals; and
- Advocacy service-learning in which students educated others on issues of public interest and the common good.

Art Chickering, David Kolb, and Alexander Astin were among the "first" to study various modes of learning as related to development of young people of secondary and college age groups. Their findings supported the anecdotal reports from students who engaged in service-learning. Since then, other faculty built on their respective theories and findings. Many graduate students based their dissertation studies on results of these leading faculty members.

In as much as service-learning advocates were affiliated with educational institutions, independent research and evaluation had been and continues to be critical to sustaining development and growth of service-learning. The quality and design of service-learning on campuses are pretty well developed. But, public and academic policies, whether at the federal, state or local level, requires further research. Should all students be "required" to have a service-learning experience or course of study? Are there areas of service where students should not engage? What might those areas be?

Some colleges and universities have adopted policies as part of their respective academic systems. Others required service-learning offerings to meet existing policies. At the federal level, most public policies dealt with federal support for various programs, such as VISTA, AmeriCorp, and so on. There are relatively few state or local public policies especially dealing with service-learning. Nor has there been much, if any, policy research to determine if there are any needs.

I know there is one area that needs attention: policies related to federal, state, and local financial aid, especially related to need-based financial assistance. Most students qualifying for need-based financial aid are required to work as partial support for getting aid. But, service-learning requires time typically used for work, during working hours, 8–5, and not after hours. Thus, many students on financial aid are not able to take on service-learning. There are precedents for exemptions and waivers. For example, to encourage teaching in urban areas, education students who teach in inner-city school for an amount of time have part of their financial aid "forgiven." Medical students who serve in rural areas may have similar waivers. But, these provisions are provided after graduation. We need something during the student tenure. There may be other areas that require more studies and the development of public policies.

So, where's the wisdom in service-learning?

- Theoretically, service-learning as a pedagogy is well developed, but needs vigilance, as both the students and community needs are dynamic and changing;
- Research and evaluation have sustained the growth of service-learning, but because of constant change, it needs to continue;
- Development of advocates for service-learning continues to be a challenge, with fewer and fewer professional organizations supporting it and few academic units adopting it as an ongoing part of their discipline;
- Public and academic policies need further research and development; and finally
- Development and sustaining service-learning need advocates to broaden their perspectives and efforts, to think outside of simply a service-learning orientation.

The foundation of service-learning has been built by many of us whose names appear in this book, and many more. Many new names have surfaced and the movement continues, building upon the foundations established by those who went before. May each generation of new service-learning advocates and participants become wiser than the previous generation in making the world a better place for humanity.

REFERENCES

Forman, B. H. (Ed.). (2011/1895). *The letters of John Keats.* Cambridge, England: Cambridge University Press.

Kaye, C. B. (2010). *The complete guide to service learning: Proven, practical ways to engage students in civic responsibility, academic curriculum, & social action.* Minneapolis, MN: Free Spirit.

Schneider, M. K. (1998, June). Models of Good Practice for Service-Learning Programs. *AAHE Bulletin, 50,* 9–12

CHAPTER 7

A TIME TO SERVE, A TIME TO LEAD

James C. Kielsmeier

There is a time for everything, and a season for every activity under heaven.
—Ecclesiastes 3:1 (NIV)

Education is not the filling of a pail but the lighting of a fire.
—William Butler Yates (Fitzhenry, 1987)

If Now—this is my Idea—there were instead of military conscription, a conscription of the whole youthful population . . . to coal mines and iron mines, to fishing fleets in November . . . to come back to society with healthier sympathies and soberer ideas.
—William James, 1906, Stanford University (James, 1910, p. 112)

Everybody can be great—because everybody can serve.
—Martin Luther King, Jr., 1968 (Washington, 1986, p. 265)

Now in my seventh decade, I'm seeking to honor this assignment to identify a few key benchmarks in a lifelong personal and professional journey. When I stepped away from day to day responsibilities as Founder/CEO of The National Youth Leadership Council in 2010 after 27 years, I anticipated that writing an inclusive retrospective would be a next assignment.

Where's the Wisdom in Service-Learning?, pages 101–114
Copyright © 2017 by Information Age Publishing
All rights of reproduction in any form reserved.

Elements of this brief chapter are drawn from that longer effort. I'm grateful now to our esteemed editor for the opportunity to pause and highlight a few personal benchmarks in my lifetime involvement in the Minnesota, national and global service-learning movements.

In particular, I have felt renewed urgency to bring attention to service-learning for younger students in the wake of the disastrous impact that stripping Federal support from the Corporation for National and Community Service in 2011 has had on service-learning. A segment of this chapter will discuss the history of this issue and suggest how and why renewal of Federal support is critical now. My hope is that this and similar efforts will inspire renewed interest for backing federal support for service-learning as a new administration takes office in 2017.

I was introduced to the power of service-learning in South Korea in 1966. A new 2nd Lieutenant trained as an Army Ranger, my platoon patrolled the hostile demilitarized zone (DMZ) separating the two Koreas. After six months I was named to lead a human relations project for the 15,000 troops of the U.S. Army's Second Infantry Division. The Second Infantry was positioned astride the historic invasion route to Seoul, and on constant alert to repel a North Korean attack.

Ironically, attitude studies showed South Korean civilians hated the Americans more than the belligerent North Koreans poised to once again invade the South. A combination of cultural insensitivity, racism, and arrogance as well as sharp contrasts in incomes and lifestyles fueled a climate of mutual disrespect between the occupying U.S. Army and our Korean hosts. The tension had boiled over into large scale pilfering of army equipment and espionage that supported North Korean agents who were in our area.

My attempts at lecturing the troops about changing their attitudes and behavior toward our Korean allies were a dismal failure. It was clear that a new plan was needed. Lieutenant Chung Young Bok, a liaison officer from the 27th Regimental Combat Team, South Korean Army, and I discovered a strategy that was effective and that introduced me to a way of teaching that would change my life.

Lt. Chung and I found a way to place American soldiers as volunteer English language tutors in all 14 Korean middle and high schools in the division area. Despite warnings from my supervisors that American soldiers would not volunteer and that we could never adequately prepare them to teach English to Korean students, 2nd Division troops volunteered in droves to tutor. We enlisted the Peace Corps to train them—a cross-cultural experience in itself for both the Army and the Peace Corps.

Participating Korean schools were delighted with the effectiveness of the new cadre of volunteer tutors. There were other indicators that our effort was bridging the cultural divide. The Korean press, usually highly critical of American troops' deportment in local communities, discovered the English

Language Assistance Program and widely publicized the story of how Korean/American goodwill was demonstrated through the tutoring partnership. The army embraced it once it proved to be successful and replicated it throughout Korea. My boss in the army, who initially condemned my plan, wrote the citation for my Army Commendation Medal.

Ten years later, in one of America's grimmest inner cities, the wisdom of combining service and cross age tutoring was again revealed. I was then based at the American Youth Foundation in St. Louis asked to prepare several hundred high school young people to mentor over 3,000 middle school students, 5 days a week, for 10 weeks of summer school. Forced integration of St. Louis area public schools and the threat of racial violence led to my hiring. The mix of Black and White young people took their positions as tutors very seriously. Training of the high school leaders began with a morning warm up aerobic exercise activity involving music and movement. Eventually, the older students in training would lead these exercises for their elementary school students.

Derek Jackson, a 16-year-old, was always there on time and very involved in the training activities. Six foot two inches tall, physically strong and determined, he looked as if he could be a tight end on the football team. One day at aerobics, I noticed Derek suddenly leave the gymnasium. I followed and found him outside sitting on the steps. When I asked him why he left training, he said that he'd been accidentally kicked. I kidded him, "What kind of excuse is that?" Derek stood up stiffly and replied, "My leg really does hurt!" He then rolled up his pants leg, exposing a jagged bleeding bullet hole in his calf.

As we drove to the hospital, Derek told me that he had been shot at a party the night before. He was afraid to say anything because he really wanted to keep the tutoring job. He said that he wanted to help younger students read. Happily, Derek's leg healed and he went on to be an outstanding leader that summer (Kielsmeier, 1998).

These experiences in Korea and St. Louis were formative in my understanding of how schools and service could be linked through the idea of service-learning. My earlier work with Outward Bound in Colorado also supported these ideas. When Outward Bound began in 1941, it had a strong service ethic. Outdoor adventure, now Outward Bound's primary identity, was, according to Outward Bound founder Kurt Hahn, preparation for a life of service—not an end in itself. Strength of character nurtured through climbing or kayaking was to be exercised through acts of compassion. Kurt Hahn's favorite example was Jesus' parable of the Good Samaritan, where, despite strong social sanctions against helping a wounded person of another culture, the Samaritan crossed the road to give aid.

The opportunity to integrate adventure and service in a new way presented itself in 1979 with the offer to build a youth leadership program in St.

Louis. An opening camp experience combined adventure, performing arts and social justice themes, then led into "back home" joint service projects for suburban White and urban Black kids, including the summer tutoring program that brought Derek Jackson to my attention. The camp became quite popular, attracting culturally diverse delegations from Indianapolis, Kansas City, Gary, New York City, Chicago, and the Cherokee Nation of Oklahoma.

Youth development pioneers Dr. Diane Hedin and Dr. Dan Conrad from the University of Minnesota evaluated the camp and found statistically significant gains on the part of participants in their willingness to contribute to society, sense of personal efficacy or empowerment, self-concept and their level of acceptance of people of different races. The light bulb went on for me: These data, collected consistently over 3 years of camp/community programming, indicated that the mix of adventure, art, social justice, and particularly service program elements led to both personal growth and the possibility of community healing during a time of racial tension.

Young people grew personally and their willingness to build just communities also grew. It was time for me to take the next step to advance the idea. A major downsizing at the American Youth Foundation moved me faster than anticipated. My job was eliminated. In March 1983, our family packed a U-Haul truck and headed for St. Paul and the University of Minnesota to teach youth studies and start the National Youth Leadership Council (NYLC).

When we arrived in Minnesota I was convinced the idea of youth service linked to schools was the right path for our work. The first few years, operating a national network of youth leadership camps was the major activity of NYLC. But young people gave feedback indicating that tackling issues of racial discrimination or environmental degradation after they left camp found little back home support among youth organizations, teachers, and school administrators. Clearly, the high-impact camp experience was not enough. A year round curricular infrastructure needed to be built to raise the level of understanding of service-learning and drive it into the fabric of our schools.

I had always been interested in nonmilitary national service such as called for by William James in his essay, *The Moral Equivalent of War* (1910). Upon leaving my required stint in the army, I thought that elements of the military should be shaped toward nonmilitary ends like the Civilian Conservation Corps of the 1930s in which my father served. It was apparent though that a new separate conservation corps-type program alone for young adults could not reach the scale needed of reaching all young people.

My conclusion: service, social justice, environmental stewardship, and compassion toward neighbor should be built into the growing-up experience of every citizen, starting in elementary school and culminating with a full-time service year. *K–12 public education had to be central to this national vision.*

NYLC with its smattering of national camps and limited research base at the University of Minnesota could not take on this vision alone. We began to focus on the State of Minnesota as a target for an integrated strategy of legislative and program initiatives.

I was asked to present the framework for a statewide service and service-learning model on November 13, 1987 at a congressional hearing chaired by Minnesota Congressman Gerry Sikorski at the State Capital in St Paul.[1] With essential support from colleague Rich Willits Cairn, I called for Minnesota to build a framework of service opportunities that "would be woven into the total fabric of growing up much as music, art and sports are integrated" (Congressional Record, 1987, p. 59). NYLC crafted a mission for the state with implications for how service-learning could be integrated into other states, the nation and larger world.

An important early step was to organize a meeting of several community leaders, including Minnesota Attorney General Hubert Humphrey III and Rick Jackson, director of the University of Minnesota YMCA, who in turn helped sponsor a two-day retreat to help promote the idea. This group pushed the 1985 Legislature to form and fund a state commission to map an integrated youth service program. Led by NYLC, a growing Minnesota movement spent the latter half of the decade developing demonstration models and building public policy support for state sponsorship of service-learning (Inskip, 1989).

Many people were drawn to Minnesota to see our state wide implementation of a comprehensive service model. We hosted a series of national working sessions and in 1989 with strong support from Governor Rudy Perpich, NYLC launched at the University of Minnesota, the first National Service-Learning Conference. After 26 years, the conference annually draws up to 2,000 people to sites rotating across the country and modeled globally in several other countries. Parallel to NYLC work in Minnesota were efforts by several national and statewide groups interested in creating a nonmilitary national service system. Leaders from state wide service and service-learning initiatives in Pennsylvania, Vermont, Massachusetts, California, and the State of Washington were especially supportive early on (Inskip, 1993).

I was invited to testify to the Senate Committee on Labor and Human Resources in 1989 to support the national Service to America Act.[2] The introduction to my testimony was motivated by the belief that American youth were ready to be challenged. I opened with a quote by a student volunteer at a home for the mentally retarded:

> This may sound strange, but through working with the women and learning to understand them, I've come closer to understanding myself. It's like while

> I'm working with them to broaden their perspective, I find myself broadening my own. In a way we're like a team. I help them and they help me and together we've gained a healthier self-concept.

I then went on to say,

> I'm compelled to offer testimony on this legislation because of what I know of people like the young woman who wrote the above in her journal. Youth service is not a vague conceptual framework of enlightened social engineering. I'm a person who worked with kids for over 25 years, a youth worker. Youth service is a hands-on reality for me, something that is good for kids—all kinds of kids, and good for America.

After years as a school teacher, soldier, wilderness instructor and college professor, I had found in the act of engaging young people in interesting, useful service for others the most powerful youth development and educational tool imaginable. In the process, I learned and grew in my respect for the incredible capacity of our younger citizens to work, create, problem solve and give. Young people are a vastly underused and under-acknowledged resource.

Convinced of the demonstrated validity of service-learning as an educational and community development process Governor Rudy Perpich championed passage of the first in the nation state legislation to fund service-learning for K–12 and higher education and opened the First National Service-Learning Conference in St. Paul in 1989. Perpich included me in a delegation to a National Governors Association annual meeting in Chicago where I met Harris Wofford. That meeting began three decades of friendship and collaboration with Harris.

In 2006, former President Bill Clinton gave Harris the first NYLC William James National Service Lifetime Achievement Award at the 17th Annual National Service-Learning Conference in Philadelphia. Along with working with President Kennedy in starting the Peace Corps and serving as U.S. Senator, Harris championed state-based service-learning in Pennsylvania while Secretary of Labor and Industry for Pennsylvania. In 1995, as CEO of the Corporation for National and Community, Harris signed an important Declaration of Principles with then Secretary of Education Richard Riley on the need to combine service and learning in public education (PDK May 2000, pp. 670–672). On April 15, 2016, Harris and I discussed next steps for national service and service-learning, including his support for bringing back funding for service-learning.

U.S. Senator David Durenberger (R-MN) also had a major impact on garnering federal support for service-learning within National and Community Service legislation and was recognized for his contributions publically at the 15th Anniversary Celebration of Learn and Serve America in

2005. Along with the late Senator Ted Kennedy, Senator Durenberger received the Congressional Founders Award.[3]

This takes us up to the launching of comprehensive Federal legislation in 1990 and 1993 that created the Corporation for National and Community Service and its signature programs: AmeriCorps, VISTA, Senior Corps, and Learn and Serve America. Senator Durenberger stood strongly with Learn and Serve from its founding believing that the non-stipended service dimension of service-learning made the overall National Service program much more attractive to fiscal conservatives with its particularly cost effective model.

Learn and Serve was a central component of the original National and Community Service Act (1990) and defunded in 2011 without public notice, hearings or discussion: reportedly in a "deal" involving the Office of Management and Budget and White House. There has never been a public explanation and perhaps because an item of around $40 million (estimated annual budget of Learn and Serve America) is considered too insignificant. What is not insignificant has been the impact particularly on K–12 and Higher Education service-learning. Among other things this funding supported a state coordinator of service-learning in nearly every state education agency.

STARTING FRESH

The need remains for renewing the Federal appropriation for service-learning. Hopefully, a new administration will consider these arguments in renewing this vital resource.

> We shall not cease from exploration, and the end of all our exploring will be to arrive where we started and know the place for the first time. (Eliot, 1943, p. 3)

Students of all backgrounds demonstrate interest and capacity to contribute to country and community. However, service opportunities are now increasingly available only in K–12 schools serving affluent communities. And too often without adherence to quality standards developed over more than two decades of practice. Most students discover meaning and purpose as they serve and are genuinely interested in "making a difference." For others however, community service and service-learning are primarily high-school graduation requirements or simply accomplishments to be noted in their quest for admission to the "right college."

Research in 2006 by Harris Interactive (Growing to Greatness [G2G], 2006), Sagawa (2010), and others has shown that engagement in quality service-learning opens social mobility doors by broadening contact with caring adults and a wider range of vocational possibilities. Adults write letters of recommendation for college and facilitate internships and summer jobs. In short, volunteer service and particularly well organized service-learning, is a pathway to increased social mobility for many students.

Who is left out? Typically, young people from predominantly low income school communities. Among them, the 94% of African American youth who attend public schools. Data has shown far more participation in service-learning among students from more affluent schools. *Access to service-learning today threatens to be a social justice and equity issue, fueled by low expectations based on race and class as much as by limited school resources.* Across the nation, funding for service-learning through Learn and Serve America had begun to increase access for low income and students of color before it was cut in 2011. (Between 1994 and 2010, over $700 million was designated by the Corporation for National and Community Service (CNCS) to K–12 schools, Tribal communities and higher education.)

Just as the expectation or frontline military service once excluded soldiers of color, a class/race service-learning apartheid threatens to further separate school communities. Without making service-learning accessible to schools and students in all zip codes this powerful tool for learning and community development can do the opposite by reinforcing separation by race and class and between haves and have nots. Starting in elementary school, engagement in service linked to curriculum establishes a base for citizen participation and active learning, while opening doors for social mobility. My belief, from the onset of my career, has been that *access to service-learning is not only about achievement and citizenship, it is a social justice issue.* Separation by race and class is reinforced when only certain people are asked to contribute and serve. This separation was clearly not what Dr. King had in mind in 1968 and why his words are so often repeated during annual celebrations of the Martin Luther King Holiday.

> And so Jesus gave us a new norm of greatness. If you want to be important—wonderful. If you want to be recognized—wonderful. If you want to be great—wonderful. But recognize that he who is greatest among you shall be your servant. That's your new definition of greatness. And this morning, the thing I like about it . . . by giving that definition of greatness, it means that everybody can be great. Because everybody can serve. You don't have to have a college degree to serve. You don't have to make your subject and your verb agree to serve. You don't have to know about Plato and Aristotle to serve. You don't have to know Einstein's theory of relativity to serve. You don't have to know the second theory of thermodynamics in physics to serve. You only need a heart full of grace. A soul generated by love. And you can be that servant. (Washington, 1986, p. 265)

I was able to confront race and class tension in the Army in South Korea in the 1960s by initiating an English tutoring program in Korean schools that brought American soldiers and Korean students together around a common cause. Later, through NYLC we worked to join mixed racial/socio economic groups together to take on shared issues. After developing relationships of trust, racially mixed groups of students can discover and work for purpose in addressing a wide range of topics—from school improvement to climate change to racial tension and more!

All young people today represent tremendous underused capacity to contribute to the common good. *However, allowing a growing pattern of exclusive race and class-based participation in service further contributes to the racial divide.* Breaking down barriers of separation by race and class should include access to improved instruction for all as well as equal opportunity to contribute through service-learning. Providing incentives through the already existing National and Community Service Act (1990) is a natural first step that must be taken by the next Administration. *Service-learning is an essential instrument to advance equity and justice (along with academic achievement and citizenship) that must start with the very young of all races and classes. After five decades this tenant remains a core component of my life work.*

RESTORE LEARN AND SERVE AMERICA

A Proposal for Discussion by Jim Kielsmeier and Jon Schroeder

Jim Kielsmeier and Jon Schroeder joined forces with other service-learning advocates—and key leaders in the Bush and Clinton administrations and Congress—to elevate the importance of service-learning in the National and Community Service legislation adopted in 1990 and 1993. At that time, Kielsmeier was founding president and CEO of the Minnesota-based National Youth Leadership Council (NYLC) and one of the nation's leading experts on service-learning. Schroeder was Senator Durenberger's Director of Policy Development and later served as an NYLC board member and board chair. Both were also founding members of Minnesota's Commission on National and Community Service, appointed by Governors Rudy Perpich (D) and Arne Carlson (R).

WHAT'S BEING PROPOSED?

This is a proposal to restore funding for the Learn and Serve America Program of the Corporation for National and Community Service. The proposal's FY2017 funding level for Learn and Serve America is $39.5 million—and is based on the program's most recent congressional appropriation in FY2010 and President Obama's budget proposals for FY2011 and 2012. To keep the Corporation's proposed budget for FY2017 at $1.1 billion, modest reductions are made in several other Corporation programs.

WHAT'S THE PROGRAM'S HISTORY?

Learn and Serve America was created by Congress in 1990 with bi-partisan support from the U.S. House and Senate and the George H. W. Bush administration. In 1993, it was expanded and incorporated into the National and Community Service Trust Act, with the leadership of the Clinton administration and, again, bi-partisan congressional support.

The 1993, legislation also created the AmeriCorp program—a high priority for President Clinton. The Corporation for National Community Service was also created as an umbrella organization for the new programs, as well as several existing programs, including VISTA, RSVP, and the Foster Grandparent program. All of these programs—including Learn and Serve America—have been reauthorized several times by Congress—most recently via the Edward M. Kennedy Serve America Act in 2009.

From 1994 to 2010, Congress appropriated more than $700.0 million for Learn and Serve America, with more than half those funds going to states on a formula to start and strengthen service-learning programs in elementary and secondary schools. The balance has been used to fund service-learning initiatives on college campuses and Indian reservations, along with research on the impacts of better funded service-learning programs and other related initiatives. Congress approved $39.5 million to fund these programs in FY2010.

SO WHY IS THIS PROPOSAL NOW NECESSARY?

After 18 years of successful operation, funding for this vital program was totally eliminated in 2011 as part of an overall budget compromise between the Obama administration and Congress. This action was a surprise since Learn and Serve had been a popular program, well received by the states. It represented just 3.5% of the Corporation's FY 2010 budget. And it was just 0.024% of discretionary spending in the Labor, HHS, Education Appropriations bill that includes the Corporation and several other independent federal agencies.

In addition, Learn and Serve America had been reauthorized just 2 years earlier in the Edward M. Kennedy Serve America Act (2009). And, in addition to the $39.5 million approved by Congress for Learn and Serve in FY2010, the program was included in President Obama's budgets for FY2011 ($40.2 million) and FY2012 ($39.5 million). This $40.2 million for Learn and Serve had also been approved by the Senate Appropriations Committee.

As "Hill Watchers" will recall, this was a time when deep partisan divisions between Congress and the president on spending and taxes had resulted in a series of "continuing resolutions" to keep the government from having to shut down. Virtually all fiscal matters were also consolidated into a single "omnibus" bill, negotiated behind closed doors by congressional leaders and top administration officials. Largely absent was the usual strong influence of each agency's leaders and appropriations subcommittee members who had deeper and historic knowledge of each of the programs being considered for cuts. Without its defenders in the room, Learn and Serve America could have been "low hanging fruit" for those holding the cutting shears—when they eventually avoided a total shutdown of all federal agencies and programs.

HOW, SPECIFICALLY, DOES THE PROPOSAL RESTORE LEARN AND SERVE FUNDING?

Regardless of how and why Learn and Serve America's funding was eliminated, authorizing language remains "alive" in the Edward M. Kennedy Serve America Act (2009). So jump-starting this vital program is as simple as restoring a line-item in the president's FY2017 budget proposal for the Corporation. That proposal is currently pending in the Labor, HHS, and Education Subcommittees of the House and Senate Appropriations Committees.

Table 7.1 shows both the previous budgets for the Corporation, the president's proposal for FY2017 and changes that would restore funding for Learn and Serve America for the fiscal year that begins October 1, 2016. In some cases, name changes were made in funding categories from year-to-year.

To keep matters as simple as possible, the proposal for restoring Learn and Serve funding totals the same $39.5 million previously approved (FY2010) and requested (FY2011–2012). In order to remain "revenue neutral" it also makes reductions elsewhere in the president's budget proposal totaling the same $39.5 million—trying to do as little damage as possible to other Corporation programs. However, if the Corporation or congressional subcommittees have better ways to make up the difference, other approaches are welcomed—as long as the $39.5 million for Learn and Serve America is retained.

TABLE 7.1 Historical Context and Proposal to Restore Funding for Learn and Serve America

Corporation Program (With Learn and Serve America Detailed)	FY2010 Appropriation	FY2011 Request[a]	FY2012 Request[a]	FY2017 Request	FY2017 Proposal[b]
AmeriCorps State and National	$372,547,000	$488,033,000	$399,790,000	$386,010,000	$372,110,000
AmeriCorps NCCC	$29,000,000	$34,593,000	$35,000,000	$30,000,000	$28,920,000
AmeriCorps VISTA	$99,074,000	$98,000,000	$100,000,000	$95,880,000	$92,428,000
State Service Commission Support Grants	$17,000,000	$18,000,000	$17,000,000	$17,000,000	$17,000,000
Learn and Serve America					
Grants	—	$38,198,000	0	0	0
School-Based Formula	$21,019,000	0	$22,541,000	0	$22,541,000
School-Based Indian Tribes and U.S.	650,000	0	697,000	0	697,000
Territories Higher Education	9,029,000	0	9,682,000	0	9,682,000
Innovation	7,417,000	0	5,810,000	0	5,810,000
Longitudinal Study	1,000,000	1,000,000	385,000	0	385,000
Grantmaking Support	385,000	0	385,000	0	385,000
Summer of Service	0	1,000,000	0	0	0
Learn and Serve America subtotal	$39,500,000	$40,198,000	$39,500,000	0	$39,500,000
Foster Grandparent Program	$110,996,000	$111,100,000	$111,100,000	$107,702,000	$107,702,000
Senior Companion Program	46,904,000	47,000,000	47,000,000	45,512,000	45,512,000
Retired Senior Volunteer Program	63,000,000	63,000,000	63,000,000	48,903,000	48,903,000
Senior Corps Subtotal	$220,900,000	$221,100,000	226,100,000	$202,117,000	$202,117,000
Social Innovation Fund	$60,500,000	$60,000,000	$70,000,000	$50,000,000	$45,000,000

(continued)

TABLE 7.1 Historical Context and Proposal to Restore Funding for Learn and Serve America (continued)					
Corporation Program (With Learn and Serve America Detailed)	FY2010 Appropriation	FY2011 Request[a]	FY2012 Request[a]	FY2017 Request	FY2017 Proposal[b]
Volunteer Generation Fund	0	$10,000,000	$5,000,000	$4,000,000	0
ServeAmerica Fellowships	0	$1,000,000	0	0	0
Innovation, Demonstration, and Other	0	$6,000,000	$5,500,000	$3,601,000	0
Evaluation	$6,000,000	$8,000,000	$6,000,000	$6,000,000	$6,000,000
Subtitle J, Training and Technical Assistance	$7,500,000	$13,000,000	$7,500,000	0	0
Disability Inclusion Grants	$5,000,000	$6,000,000	$5,000,000	0	0
National Service Trust	$197,000,000	$293,662,000	$235,326,000	$206,842,000	$200,000,000
Salaries and Expenses	$88,000,000	$109,000,000	$97,694,000	$89,330,000	$87,705,000
Office of the Inspector General	$7,700,000	$9,000,000	$8,450,000	$6,100,000	$6,100,000
Total	$1,149,721,000	$1,297,586,000	$1,257,860,000	$1,096,880,000	$1,096,880,000

[a] Overlapping requests were made for FY 2011 and FY 2012 since spending was being authorized on short-term Continuing Resolutions while efforts were made to agree on appropriations levels for both years. In the end, no appropriations were approved for Learn and Serve America for FY 2011 and 12, so the most recent Congressional appropriation was for FY 2010. However, some funds were made available to continue FY 2010 appropriations during FY 2011, under these Continuing Resolutions

[b] Corporation for National and Community Service, 2016.

NOTES

1. Commission on Federal Voluntary Service Opportunities for Young People Act of 1987. Hearing before the Subcommittee on Human Resources, November 13, 1987 (statement by James C. Kielsmeier).
2. *Hearing before the Committee on Labor and Human Resources, United States Senate*, (1989) (statement by James C. Kielsmeier).
3. Learn and Serve America 15th Anniversary Symposium and Celebration, Corporation for National and Community Service, Washington, D.C, December 2005.

REFERENCES

Congressional Record. (1987). Commission on Federal Voluntary Service Opportunities for Young People Act of 1987, Hearing before Subcommittee on Post Office and Civil Service, House of Representatives, HR 3096, a Bill to Establish a Commission to Study Federal Service Opportunities for Young People. Convened by Hon Gerry Sikorski, Minnesota November 13, 1987

Edward M. Kennedy Serve America Act, 42 U.S.C. § 12501 (2009).

Eliot, T. S. (1943). *Four quartets.* New York, NY: Harcourt.

Every Student Succeeds Act, 20 U.S.C. § 6301 (2015).

Fitzhenry, R. (1987). *Barnes and Noble book of quotations.* New York, NY: Barnes and Noble Books.

Growing to Greatness (G2G). (2006). Retrieved from http://www.peecworks.org/peec/peec_research/01795BFB-001D0211.1/growing%20to%20greatness%202006.pdf

Inskip, L. (1989, June 11). Commentary. *Minnesota Star Tribune.* Retrieved from http://www.startribune.com/

James, W. (1910). "The Moral Equivalent of War." International Conciliation, N. 27.

Kielsmeier, J. (1993, July 6). Editorial: Minnesota cooperates, leads on youth service. *Minneapolis Star Tribune.*

Kielsmeier, J. (1998). To Be of Service: The grassroots initiative of service-learning in the United States. *Zip Lines: The Voice for Adventure Education, 37*(Fall), 19–23.

National and Community Service Act, 42 U.S.C. § 12501 (1990).

Sagawa, S. (2010). *The American way to change: How national service and volunteers are transforming America.* San Francisco, CA: Josey Bass.

Washington, J. M. (Ed.). (1986). *The Essential Writings and Speeches of Martin Luther King, Jr.* San Francisco, CA: Harper Collins.

CHAPTER 8

THE WISDOM OF TERRY PICKERAL

Terry Pickeral

THE EARLY YEARS

I was raised in a family that not only valued service but ensured it became a habit. I can remember at a very young age joining my parents and others to contribute to those in need and acknowledge we were part of a community and that service was an expected activity. No questions asked.

Throughout my life I tried to practice providing service to others and when my father passed away early in my life, we received service from others until we "landed on our feet." What goes around comes around.

During my adolescence and late teens I spent less time serving others but never forgot that the ethic of service was part of my DNA. It wasn't until 1989 when I managed a campus-based summer program for at-risk middle school students that I incorporated service as a core experience of each student. We worked with community environmental groups in local wetlands projects that demonstrated to our students they have value and can contribute to community development. Several of our teachers demonstrated to me that the service students performed could be integrated into our math, science and language arts classes and I encouraged them to connect the service to the classroom.

Where's the Wisdom in Service-Learning?, pages 115–127
Copyright © 2017 by Information Age Publishing
All rights of reproduction in any form reserved.

In 1990, I was asked by Campus Compact to share these early campus-based experiences of young people with others under the concept of mentoring. As I explained to diverse audiences (teachers, education leaders, state policymakers, and youth advocates) that I merely engaged students in service to their community and our teachers connected their efforts to their curriculum. I did not think we were actually mentoring but engaging students in ways to demonstrate their attributes, skills and talents in a community setting by doing meaningful service.

Once I shared our stories I was informed by service-learning advocates that I was actually engaged in service-learning. I was not aware of the concept, nor that there was a national network of advocates and that many others were conducting similar work in schools and communities nationwide.

I remember my first National Youth Leadership Council Service-Learning National Conference in Orlando, Florida where I began to understand that there was a collection of practitioners, and unlike other conferences, there were many students not just attending, but facilitating workshops.

This enlightenment served as a springboard to advancing service-learning beyond one campus-based program for middle school students to a wide set of activities based on service-learning philosophy, frameworks and effective practices.

TRANSITIONS

After those experiences we developed the Washington State Campus Compact and a whole set of service-learning activities on the Western Washington University campus engaging many university students.

My focus was three-fold:

1. Building the leadership capacity of university students to design, implement, and sustain service-learning on the campus and with local K–12 schools;
2. Building the knowledge and skills of university faculty to integrate service-learning into their courses and programs; and
3. Advancing service-learning in local K–12 schools through the collaboration with the university and the leadership of university students.

These three interconnected sets of work engaged faculty, university students, K–12 teachers and their students in service-learning moving this philosophy and pedagogy to the core of the institutions and instilling an ethic of service and service-learning in youth.

We did face challenges implementing service-learning including:

1. Finding and sharing research that showed the positive impact service-learning had on university and K–12 students.
2. Assisting university faculty and K–12 teachers to understand service-learning as an effective pedagogy rather than a teaching and learning method that could be implemented occasionally and without gaining new knowledge and skills.
3. Forging high-quality partnerships with local community organizations, groups and advocates that were mutually beneficial and required the community to be co-educators as well as places of service for university and K–12 students.
4. Securing funding for professional development, service-learning resources and transportation for K–12 schools in support of service-learning.
5. Creating and implementing a theory of change that framed our work and developed a path and timeline for implementation.
6. Finding champions to advance service-learning on campus, in K–12 schools and in the local community.
7. Articulating to diverse audiences (including parents) the philosophy, practice, outcomes, and positive impacts of service-learning (with limited research and evaluation).
8. Staying current and contributing to the national service-learning movement by participating in conferences, forums, events and broad-based activities and conversations.

Similar to my choice to have one foot in the university and the other in K–12 schools (while engaging the local community), I also developed local and national networks of colleagues to support my service-learning knowledge and skills. National Youth Leadership Council, Campus Compact, RMC Research, and Brandeis University leaders and staff were valuable in developing my attributes and capacity to advance service-learning by sharing their resources, their research, their experiences, and their insights. Similarly, local and state campus and K–12 school-based networks, along with their communities, served as a more local network of colleagues in support of my development.

Along the same time, the National Corporation for National and Community Service was developed and provided a national voice, resources, funding, and opportunities to convene and share experiences and insights.

The Washington State Campus Compact provided statewide opportunities for campus leaders, staff and students to share their strategies, challenges, and resources deepening and broadening service-learning on their campus and communities.

I was able to transition my experiences and attributes to the national level by working with the Campus Compact National Center for Community Colleges to design and implement a 2-year college service-learning initiative *From the Margin to the Mainstream* on six campuses. We were able to make significant progress on campuses through professional development, resource development, dissemination, and advocacy.

Each of the 2-year colleges built on existing service-learning programs, with a focus on deepening current work and broadening faculty development beyond the initial pioneers and advocates. We focused on sustainability as an outcome rather than merely increasing the number of faculty and students engaged in service-learning so that service-learning became a long-term large-scale campus initiative.

Building on all of my experiences, I then headed to the Education Commission of the States, and with the leadership of Frank Newman, co-developed the National Center for Learning and Citizenship (NCLC). We modeled NCLC after Campus Compact and invited state and district leaders to join a national movement to advance service-learning on K–12 schools throughout the nation.

These state and district leaders contributed to the service-learning movement by focusing on rationales, what works, and how to engage students in service-learning, leading to student attributes, school improvement, and community development. We made significant progress encouraging other state, district, and school leaders to consider, adopt, and adapt high-quality service-learning into their schools and effectively engage students as leaders.

We conducted the initial 50-state service-learning policy scan identifying existing policies in support of service-learning and policy options for states, districts, and schools to consider, adopt, and/or adapt. Our progress led to NCLC's selection as a partner in the W. K. Kellogg Foundation *Learning in Deed* national service-learning initiative. We worked with five states and their schools to decrease service-learning policy impediments, increase policy supports, increase prevalence of high-quality service-learning practice and increase infrastructure in support of service-learning.

In addition, Learning in Deed established a national service-learning commission to be a national voice, a research team to conduct and share lessons learned and implications from research, resource development to inform and influence education stakeholders and advance a service-learning movement from the initial champions to a broader base of advocates and practitioners.

Ultimately, Learning in Deed led to a focus on sustainability and advancing service-learning as a core expectation of each student. We examined sustainability, focusing on other education topics/issues and our efforts in the five states to develop the following sustainability framework:

- Vision and Leadership
  - A diverse group of stakeholders have a shared vision and leadership opportunities
- Curriculum
  - The structures and frameworks to develop and revise curriculum
- Professional Development
  - Administrators, faculty, staff and others have regular opportunities to engage in training and to create a community of practice
- Partnerships and Community
  - School-community partnerships benefit schools, students, and community
- Continuous Improvement
  - Formalized opportunities for analyzing data for continuous improvement

We developed a set of resources for states, districts, schools and service-learning advocates based on these five sustainability elements that include specific examples of what it looks like in schools and what it takes for schools to sustain high-quality service-learning.

I do want to make it clear that while we provided nominal funds to schools, we emphasized that they had a responsibility to support high-quality service-learning through policies, resources, support, and alignment; otherwise, service-learning would be vulnerable and obviously not sustainable. Reliance on external, funding rather than fully integrating service-learning into a school, reduces school ownership and a commitment to sustainability.

As NCLC advanced its work, there was a purposeful change from a focus on service-learning to a focus on civic development and examining how service-learning was an effective strategy for students to gain civic knowledge, skills, and dispositions. This shift broadened service-learning contributions in schools building on our previous years' efforts solely on service-learning.

As part of the Education Commission of the States we had access to policymakers and education leaders and we were able to demonstrate how service-learning and civic development aligned with and/or enhanced existing education initiatives and priorities. We were provided forums to engage these policymakers and education leaders, demonstrating the benefits of service-learning and adoptable/adaptable policies and practices.

In addition, NCLC was selected to assist particular states to examine service-learning and civic development. One example was our work with the Mississippi Department of Education's focus on systemic renewal following the destruction of Hurricane Katrina. We contributed to a statewide dropout prevention program focusing on student engagement using our service-learning and civic development frameworks and strategies to solicit insights from students in every school throughout Mississippi. This successful initiative demonstrated that service-learning frameworks applied to and had implications for other education issues, challenges, and opportunities.

This is not a nominal finding, but rather a demonstration of the power of service-learning as an effective strategy to address major education issues such as dropout prevention, school climate, student engagement, parent/family engagement, and community engagement.

Speaking of school climate, this is another education issue where we employed service-learning frameworks focusing on the quality and character of schools. Along with the National School Climate Center we developed a national school climate initiative focusing on school safety, trusting relationships, pedagogy, and physical environment. It was a logical connection between service-learning and these school climate elements.

In 2008, I departed NCLC and began a journey with Special Olympics and their new Project UNIFY school-based initiative. I was selected to contribute to this initiative given my experience in service-learning and student engagement. It was immediately evident that these frameworks logically connected to integrating social inclusion in schools throughout the United States.

This is another example of how service-learning frameworks apply to multiple education and social justice topics. At the same time America's Promise Alliance developed a national dropout prevention initiative focusing on service-learning, we were engaged with this initiative providing service-learning professional development to district and school leaders in 12 urban cities to increase school integration of service-learning.

About this time, I reduced my focus on service-learning and increased my commitment to student engagement. This transition built on my decades of experience in service, service-learning, and civic development leading to a recognition that student engagement needs to be supported by engaging pedagogy, school climate, and adult support (all elements of high-quality service-learning).

As I focused on student engagement I found the framework developed by my colleague Anderson Williams to be an effective guide for my work and offered the best continuum for assessing and improving student engagement.

Anderson created a continuum with student participation as the first stage leading to student voice that leads to student leadership and then to student engagement. In addition, he includes the responsibilities of adults to support the various stages of student engagement that is essential to encouraging, supporting, and sustaining student engagement (Figure 8.1).

This section is titled *Transitions* to share my journey from service to service-learning to student engagement, all based on the core tenet that we need to provide high-quality opportunities for each student to contribute

PARTICIPATION ➡	VOICE ➡	LEADERSHIP ➡	ENGAGEMENT
YOUTH ROLES Youth are involved in the "doing" of the activity but not in the planning, development or reflection.	Youth are part of conversations regarding planning and implementing an idea. Their input is considered, but they may or may not have an official "vote".	Youth are involved at all levels of idea or project development and have formal and informal leadership roles in the process.	Youth are the primary drivers of the work from conceptualization to implementation and reflection. Youth "own" and understand the work deeply.
ADULT ROLES Adults develop the idea, plan and organize all aspects of the activity or event which a cadre of young people will actually carry out.	Adults develop and set the agenda. Adults include the input of youth in this process. This can be through consideration of youth input via focus group or meeting or through youth being involved in and having a formal vote.	Adults are involved in the full process and support the development of individual youth and the flow of the process, but in a way that balances power and leadership with youth. Adults allow youth to struggle and make mistakes in a safe environment.	Adults provide a support role and share ownership and commitment but with some deference to the youth. Adults hold one "vote" on the team.
DECISION-MAKING Adults make all decisions.	Adults ultimately make the decision with the consideration of youth input. If youth have a vote, they are typically outnumbered or adults have ultimate veto power.	Youth and adults share decision-making power often requiring a specific and mutually agreed upon decision-making process.	Youth ultimately make the decisions with the inclusion of adult input and "vote".

Figure 8.1 Understanding the continuum of youth involvement.

to their own development, their school's improvement, and their community's development. The result is that each student will acquire and enhance their academic, civic and career knowledge and skills; expand their social emotional competencies; focus on their individual as well as their social responsibilities; and integrate active principled citizenship into their lives.

UPON REFLECTION

As I reflect on my journey into and out of service-learning, one specific question continues to come to my mind: Is service-learning a field, a movement, or something else?

Once I learned about and then engaged in service-learning, I wondered if it was truly a field, as for me an education or academic field is a branch of knowledge that is commonly defined, recognized by schools, and supported by research. Despite noble attempts and strategies, I am not sure service-learning meets my criteria.

So if service-learning is not a field, then perhaps it is a movement. To me, a movement is a set of actions by a group of individuals and organizations focused on a specific political or social issue. In addition, movements required a strategic communication strategy, creating and sustaining networks, maximizing current leaders, and developing a set of emerging leaders.

I think service-learning is challenged to articulate its message, which may be a function of diverse understandings of what service-learning is: Is it an engaging pedagogy for students to acquire and enhance academic knowledge and skills? A school-based practice leading to civic competencies? A school and community partnership focused on student development, school improvement, and community development? Or a combination of these three, or something else?

Do service-learning advocates effectively network with the core individuals and organizations to advance its work? I acknowledge there have been high-quality collaborations with national and state education and social organizations to integrate service-learning into their agendas, but far too often being invited to their table does not lead to changing the conversation in favor of student engagement and contributions being a high priority supported by advocacy, policy and practice.

What about maximizing current service-learning leaders? In 2001 the Learning in Deed initiative developed The National Service-Learning Partnership, as an advocacy organization committed to promoting service-learning in schools and communities across the country. This group was enhanced by the National Commission on Service-Learning, engaging national political and education leaders (including one young person) to inform and influence policymakers, practitioners, and community partners. This was one attempt to mobilize service-learning leaders and I know there were others, many of them in response to federal funding requests or federal funding elimination. To my knowledge mobilizing service-learning leaders has not led to significant progress for it to become a core expectation of each student.

What about creating a set of emerging service-learning leaders? One of the strategies I recognized as I became oriented to service-learning was the engagement of youth as leaders, and I know several national organizations focus on developing youth leadership and advocacy. These strategies are to be celebrated; however, I am not sure what impact emerging leaders have had to advocate for service-learning.

So, if service-learning is not a field and is not a movement, what is it? I think service-learning, done well, is an effective strategy to engage students in service to their community: building habits of contributing, enhancing academic knowledge and skills, raising civic competencies, and promoting moral and ethical judgment.

One of the most critical elements of service-learning, given my definition above, is the intentionality of implementation. If we value service-learning to build academic knowledge and skills, then both the service and the learning need to focus on those academic outcomes; to raise civic competencies, then the service and learning need to focus on policies and politics; and if we expect service-learning to lead to moral and ethical judgment, we need to focus the service and learning on social justice causes and effective solutions.

Please make no mistake, I have learned and benefited from my engagement with service-learning. The focus on student assets rather than deficiencies guides my work; trusting relationships between students and adults in schools expands my knowledge of intergenerational leadership; focusing on using data for continuous improvement raises my appreciation for research; and following reflective practices increases my ability to learn from my experiences. These attributes, which I have applied to education issues and settings outside of service-learning, built on my earliest habits of service and elevated my ability to be effective as a team member, family member, worker and citizen.

THE WISDOM

Given that wisdom comes from practical experience and corresponding reflection, here are things I have learned from my years working in schools and communities; with students, teachers and school leaders; with state policymakers and education leaders of all ages; and with national education and social organizations and networks.

First, I am an advocate for asking essential questions, those are questions that are broad and timeless, point to big ideas and make sense of complicated issues.

According to Grant Wiggins (2007) a question is essential when it:

1. Causes genuine and relevant inquiry into the big ideas and core content;
2. Provides deep thought, lively discussion, sustained inquiry and new understanding as well as more questions;
3. Requires consideration of alternatives, weighing evidence, supporting others' ideas and justifying answers;
4. Stimulates vital, on-going rethinking big ideas, assumptions and prior learning;
5. Sparks meaningful connections with prior learning and personal experiences; and
6. Naturally recurs, creating opportunities for transfer to other situations and topics.

Thus, my service-learning journey and transition has been informed by essential questions such as:

1. Are there pressing current or emerging issues that merit consideration for service-learning?
2. What are the questions for which service-learning is the answer?
3. To what extent does power or lack of power affect teachers and students?
4. What are the responsibilities of an individual in regard to issues of social justice?
5. When is it appropriate to challenge the beliefs and values of society? Of schools?

I find my answers and deliberations with others inform my decisions, my work and my advocacy. Service-learning advocates can consider using essential questions similarly to advance and enhance their advocacy.

Second, connected to my earlier point of whether service-learning is a field, a movement or a set of practices and programs I believe examining what service-learning advocates most value about service-learning and organize work focused on those values. Once determining what service-learning is at this level advocates can mount a campaign using the strategies connected to field, movement or other work. For example if service-learning is an effective pedagogy for learning course content then mobilize a campaign demonstrating, through high-quality research, this connection and the implications for national, state and local policy, practice, and capacity/infrastructure.

Third, I believe that finding and engaging champions to advocate for service-learning at the federal, state, local, and/or school level is a necessary first step, but from my experience, we need to also cultivate the next generation of advocates ensuring long-term and large-scale implementation and sustainability. Too often, we rely on the initial champions (pioneers) and fail to move beyond them. This is a delicate dance, but a necessary one if service-learning is to thrive in our schools and communities.

Fourth, policy matters to effectively support and sustain service-learning. In my early years in service-learning when I advocated for policy I was often told, "We do not need any more policies." Well I believe we do need policies as they set the goals, direction, priorities, resources, and accountability systems to successfully integrate and sustain service-learning. We need to move advocates to lead policy efforts rather than react to policies; policymaking is an art and a science but engaging in policymaking should be a priority for a successful field or movement. Perhaps we confuse policy with lobbying but informing and influencing policymakers is a critical democratic strategy.

Fifth, research is a critical component of successful service-learning both for researchers and advocates: researchers asking the right questions, collecting data from all education stakeholders, analyzing the data and showing the implications; and advocates need to use research to continuously improve to understand and create the conditions necessary in schools for service-learning to be effective and sustainable.

Sixth, I have mentioned sustainability throughout my service-learning journey and transition and believe service-learning advocates need to ensure their efforts focus on increasing the prevalence of high-quality service-learning, policy supports, and capacity/infrastructure to support. This is not unique to service-learning, as we can point to other education topics/ issues such as instructional technology that have moved from the school's margins to its core.

Seventh, readiness is a real factor in whether an individual, an organization, and/or a network effectively embrace service-learning. Individuals, organizations, and networks have their own values, culture, and practices and their readiness to integrate service-learning is variable. Conducting research, asking questions and other due diligence strategies, can predict interest, capacity, and willingness to integrate service-learning. In addition, service-learning advocates can continuously move individuals, organizations, and networks along a continuum of readiness by sharing service-learning research, stories, and benefits.

Eighth, each student has a story and asking them questions about their experiences, as well as seeking their insights, are critical to understanding student interests, gifts, and talents. These student assets are effective building blocks for student empowerment and service-learning. Talking with students, surveying students, and engaging students in action research yield data we can analyze and integrate into our schools and communities for student development, school improvement, and community enhancement.

TOWARD THE NEXT 40 YEARS

For young leaders today to successfully sustain high-quality service-learning, I offer the following suggestions that engage students, teachers, staff, administrators, families, and communities.

1. Expand student engagement throughout P-K systems focusing on each student's assets, interests and talents toward positive individual, school and community contributions. Acknowledging that each student is capable of providing services connected to their academic, social-emotional, civic and career development through creating strategies that ask students to share their experiences, insights and interests and act on their ideas for service-learning activities and reflections.

2. Ensure teacher preparation programs include service-learning in their overview of the teaching profession, methods courses and

student teaching practica. This includes the alignment of service-learning within all subject areas and with all student groupings. This includes school staff and leader training so that all adults in schools have the knowledge, skills and dispositions to effectively integrate service-learning into the core of the school.

3. Focus on school policies, priorities, practices and infrastructure to ensure service-learning is an expectation and experience of each student and part of the accountability system. This includes hiring policies, professional development, evaluation and continuous improvement to ensure service-learning is core to the school system.

4. Ensure there are high-quality effective ways for parent engagement in schools. This requires schools to acknowledge that parents have different school experiences, attitudes, and aptitudes to engage with the school thus requiring diverse engagement strategies.

5. Focus on school climate to ensure the quality and character of the school not only accommodates service-learning, but in fact expects service-learning to be a daily activity throughout school. School climate should be measured, ensuring each education stakeholder shares their experiences and expectations, analyzed and continuously improved to ensure service-learning is supported and sustained.

6. Promote community engagement so that individuals, groups, organizations and networks serve as co-educators as well as places of serving and learning for students. This includes inviting others to engage in service-learning by creating specific mutually beneficial expectations and responsibilities for them and the students and school. Through these partnerships students are able to see the relevance of education, develop aspirations, understand how the community operates and examine their contributions to community development.

7. Ensure a focus on sustainability so that each student, teacher, staff, leaders, and partners are engaged in service-learning. Develop policies that encourage, support and reward service-learning and provide the resources and infrastructure to ensure service-learning is an expectation and experience of each student. Align service-learning with the school's mission, priorities and accountability system so there is an overt and intentional commitment to service-learning.

CONCLUSION

Engaging in service at an early age set me on a journey that led me to service-learning many years ago. My service-learning experiences enhanced my knowledge, skills, and dispositions as an advocate, as well as question how service-learning is organized, supported, and successfully implemented in schools and communities.

My career path has been informed by service-learning values, frameworks, and networks that have been generalizable to other education and social issues in our nation.

I shared eight specific things I have learned (wisdom I have gained) as they have guided me in my work and life and perhaps offer some insights and implications for others to examine service-learning and its multiple benefits to individuals, schools, and communities. Finally, I offer a look to the next 40 years and offer seven suggestions for today's service-learning advocates to consider, adopt, and/or adapt.

REFERENCES

Wiggins, G. (2007, November 15). *What is an essential question?* Big Ideas: An Authentic Education e-journal. Retrieved from http://www.authenticeducation.org/ae_bigideas/article.lasso?artid=53

CHAPTER 9

WHERE'S THE WISDOM IN SERVICE-LEARNING?

My Story

Rob Shumer

MY BACKGROUND

I started teaching in 1969. I taught reading and was learning about doing Language Experience stories. Using such stories was a way to develop reading materials that were familiar to the reader because they use words in their own oral vocabulary as they tell their story. My high school students hated reading, hated school, and were in many ways not interested in formal education. Just by chance I had a friend who was teaching in an elementary school near my high school, so I decided to see if I could take my high school students to work with the first graders so they could tell my students stories as a way of teaching my students to read and write (improve their spelling). So, the first graders would tell stories, my students would write them down, and then take the stories and write them on large print paper so the elementary kids could read them. In the meantime, the first graders would draw pictures to illustrate the stories and then learn how to make books that contained their stories and pictures. My students would

Where's the Wisdom in Service-Learning?, pages 129–141
Copyright © 2017 by Information Age Publishing
All rights of reproduction in any form reserved.

learn to spell the words and would also read the stories and the other books in the elementary school (many of my students read at the 3rd to 5th grade level) so the elementary school books were easy for them . . . and helped build confidence and practice.

What was important in this activity was the noticeable difference in my students' attitudes toward school, toward reading, toward themselves, and toward me. They found the experience to be kind of fun and a break from the routine of school. We would go to the elementary school every other week; the elementary students would come to our campus on the odd weeks. What happened is my students developed relationships with the first graders. They felt needed, especially when a first grader would cry if his high school buddy wouldn't show up for the weekly exchange. They felt the work was meaningful because they were helping a child to read. As one of my students said: "I don't want them to grow up to be like me/us [not being able to read]."

I didn't know this was service-learning. I never heard of it in any of my teacher education courses. But, it turns out, it was a great example of a good service-learning program . . . .met all the criteria for meeting community needs, allowing youth voice, etc. It was transformational for many of my students, especially those who had been problem students themselves because they got to see what life was like from a teacher's point of view. As another of my students said when he was trying to direct a group of five first graders and they weren't listening to him: "Am I like this, Rob? Do I make you feel frustrated when I don't do what you ask . . . just like these kids make me feel frustrated when I can't get them to do what I need them to do?" It changed his whole perception of what being in school was like . . . .and he vowed to change his behavior to be less of a bother to teachers and his fellow students.

I start my story with this information because it changed my life. It made me realize how important it was to do meaningful work, to develop relationships with others in a helping manner, and to break the routine of schooling and classrooms. I never taught in a traditional way after that, having the opportunity to be a librarian and work with students in a supportive way, to be a work experience coordinator/counselor to help young people get connected to real people in the working world so they could see what they do, and then run an alternative program in a high school where students spent a majority of their time in community settings doing career connected work, infusing academic learning with real world learning, and seeing how constructivist curriculum (developed through the Experience Based Career Education models) could make any interest spring to life as an academic program.

My involvement in this work led me to interact with people on the national level through the regional educational laboratories (Far West, Northwest,

RBS, and Appalachian Lab) and to get a taste of what a movement was like through the EBCE program development. I met people from around the country and got involved in a national movement. I later became the president of the National EBCE Association and had the opportunity as a high school teacher to actually go to national conferences and participate in events that took me all over the country. This was never planned as a career path ... it just happened as I met people and opportunities developed.

All this work led me to think about doing a doctoral study on experiential learning. I connected with people at UCLA, notably Harry Silberman, who was a big name in vocational education and an "expert" on experiential learning programs. This connection led me to meet Ron Bloom at the Drew Medical School who was developing an experiential high school in Watts, California and needed assistance in creating the school. I joined with the Drew School and helped create the King Drew Medical Magnet High School, a school that was adjacent to the King Drew Medical Center and utilized the entire medical community to teach about all the subjects in a traditional high school, but in the context of health sciences.

I went on to do a lot of other things that led me to the place I am today—someone who has been in a multitude of roles that affected my perception of service-learning, of educational reform, and of changes in education over the past 45 years. I believe my perspective is fairly unique to the field because I have had so many roles. I share them here so you get a grounding in my perspective on education and on the world. As mentioned, I became the president of the National EBCE Association, leading a large group of vocational/career education people and programs around the United States. Through that role, as the EBCE organization began to decline, I became a member of the National Society for Internships and Experiential Education. I brought a secondary school perspective to an organization that was primarily made up of higher education folks. I later joined the board of directors for NSIEE, then as an Assistant Director and Director of Field Studies Development at UCLA. So that role had me work with more than 30 departments at a major university trying to include field based learning in the academic program .... and represent that perspective on the NSIEE organization (which was responsible for some of the early publications on the topic).

I then went on to work at the University of Minnesota as the founding Director of the National Service-Learning Clearinghouse, the largest source of information on service-learning in the nation (and in the world). We collected over 4,000 documents dealing with elementary, secondary, higher education, and community-based programs and developed a series of material/publications that told what we knew about the service-learning field. This lasted from 1994 to 2000.

During that time, I also worked with research efforts to study the Minnesota National Service program (Americorps) for 5 years. I also did research on teacher education and service-learning and even conducted a Delphi study on the meaning of service-learning. I also did research on people who were most influential/most published in the field. In addition, I worked with the Association for Supervision and Curriculum Development (ASCD) and the National Council of Social Studies (NCSS) as we developed special interest groups in the two organizations. I later became a member of the Research Advisory Group for the NCSS.

Following that work, I conducted several research studies on various programs across the country. I studied service-learning and character education in Connecticut for three years. I evaluated the Mississippi Community, Higher Education, School Partnership (CHESP) program for 2 years. I studied the Pennsylvania Service-Learning Alliance state effort, evaluating the elementary, secondary, and college projects in the state from 2002–2004.

After that, I became the first vice-chair of the International Association for Research on Service-Learning and Community Engagement, involved in research reviews of higher education. I worked with the board for several years and involved people from China, Hong Kong, Singapore, Mexico, and Ireland on various projects.

I have also conducted research on developing a self-assessment system for service-learning (primarily K–12), as well as doing a civic engagement audit for Metropolitan State University in St. Paul, Minnesota. This analysis presented an entire framework for examining the nature and scope of civic engagement at a university.

During my time in education I have also served on a variety of boards that address community issues. From the American Red Cross in Los Angeles, to the University YMCA in Minneapolis, to the Crohn's and Colitis Foundation of America, I have worked with community groups to develop service-learning efforts and community projects that link youth with the community. This connection has supported my other work with the University of Minnesota School of Social Work around issues of youth development and youth participatory evaluation. In fact, my experience has connected me with the American Evaluation Association where I served as the vice president and president of the Minnesota state chapter for 2 years. I am a member of the AEA Topical Interest Group on youth participatory/empowerment evaluation and have regularly presented at the annual AEA conference on topics related to service-learning and youth led evaluation.

Related to this work, I have also edited an online journal on service-learning research dealing with children and youth. *The Information for Action: Research on Service-Learning With Children and Youth* journal was funded for 3 years by the W. K. Kellogg Foundation and produced research articles by academics, practitioners, and even youth, themselves. The project lost funding in 2009.

I also served for several years as the internal evaluator for the National Research Center for Career and Technical Education. In addition to that work, I conducted two national studies of Programs of Study (career education) and led a national institute on developing Programs of Study with three states and Guam.

I have been doing research and program development in various countries, notably China and Singapore. I had worked in Mexico, Germany, Canada, England, Japan, and South Korea on various projects and presentations.

Throughout all this time, I have taught courses at UCLA, University of Minnesota, and Metropolitan State. The topics have covered service-learning, curriculum development, participatory evaluation, teacher education, work-based learning, career education, youth development, and experiential learning.

Suffice to say, I've spent time in all levels of education and in the community, as well as working as a teacher, faculty member, researcher, writer, presenter, and colleague. So when I comment about the highs and lows of service-learning over the past 40 years, my lens is framed by these experiences.

Because of all these activities I might categorize myself, on the social capital framework, as a "bridger." That is a person who works to connect people and "bonding" groups so they can learn and grow from and with each other. To me, making links between these various perspectives helps to identify the really big ideas and concepts that are fundamental to service-learning and good education.

THE BEST OF TIMES

I would suggest that one of the highlights of the service-learning movement was a meeting held in the early 1990s in Washington, DC convened by the Corporation for National Service. It was coordinated by Susan Stroud (an early director of the Learn and Serve program and original director of Campus Compact), Jeremy Rifkin (an economist who wrote *The End of Work: The Decline of the Global Labor Force and the Dawn of the Post-Market Era* [1995], among other books), and Jim Kielsmeier, from the National Youth Leadership Council. What was extraordinary about the meeting was the intent and the people who attended. The goal was to develop dialogue among and between the major educational reform efforts in the country and to create a discussion that would probe the place of service-learning in the educational world. People who attended, among others were Henry Levin of the Accelerated Schools movement, a representative from the Yale Center on Youth Development (Robert Sternberg's group), a representative from the

Coalition for Essential Schools (Theodore Sizer), Don Ernst from ASCD (with a Bill Clinton connection), Mac Hall, from the Native American Indian Youth Leadership program, Kate McPherson, from the Northwest Laboratory and programs in Washington and Oregon states, and several others representing other national groups.

The conversation was stimulating . . . and raised the level of understanding of where service-learning had been and where it might go in the future. Perhaps one of the most poignant comments that I recollect from the meeting was one from Henry Levin, who said that if "you thought service-learning was a new idea, you didn't understand what happened in one-room school houses throughout the 19th century."

What made the meeting so important was its intent on bringing service-learning into the mainstream of educational reform. People had always viewed it as a program on the margins of education, with the focus always on classroom based learning, with occasional forays into the community for service, for vocational learning, and for internships and apprenticeships. But community-connected, service oriented actions and learning were still considered more beneficial for personal development of the student than for serious academic learning.

The meeting helped to stimulate discussion and collaboration for the next several years, especially at the K–12 levels. There was on-going participation of service-learning individuals in ASCD, NCSS, and the American Association of School Principals (an administrator organizations).

The meeting also served to highlight the importance of maintaining a connection with the political process unfolding in the country. Clearly, connections with the federal entity responsible for promoting service-learning was very important to its livelihood and sustainability, and holding the meeting in Washington helped to promote those contacts.

Perhaps another major high for the service-learning world was the enactment of the CHESP program. As I mentioned earlier, I evaluated the state program in Mississippi and was able to learn of the great impact and purpose of the effort. I was also able to observe, first hand, the kinds of positive outcomes that were derived from the program.

First, the model for the program seemed to emphasize the essential elements of any good service-learning initiative: active collaboration between all critical areas of a setting to maximize the kind of learning and impact that could occur from a program. Research has continuously shown that the major challenges with service-learning were time, collaboration, and ability to measure its impact. In the CHESP programs all three entities, community, schools, and higher education, were required to work together on a common project. They had to include designs for program implementation and for program assessment. They leveraged the human resources of each sector to build on the efforts of each other and provided ample opportunity for service to be delivered among and between each group.

In one of the programs I evaluated, the high school students were involved in helping community members assist in the assessment of the program. The college students collaborated on the implementation and assessment and provided guidance to the high school students on their work. And the community members provided direction and feedback to make the service relevant and impactful.

One of the important outcomes of the effort was the transformation of the high school students. They reported that engagement in the evaluation portion helped to change their perspective on all programs . . . they began to question and organize actions and feedback so they knew how they were doing. They said they started to use this approach in almost everything they worked on.

One of the side effects of this effort in Mississippi was in the professional growth and development of the staff. One individual, Tom Schnaubelt, who was conducting a study of faculty involvement on the project, learned a great deal about the role and functions of faculty in effective service-learning. Tom went on to direct other programs in Mississippi, then moved to direct programs and a state effort in Wisconsin, and is currently directing the program at the Haas Center at Stanford University. Tom is considered one of the leading experts on service-learning in the country, so the opportunities afforded him through the CHESP effort had great impact on his professional development and on the field of service-learning.

The director of the Mississippi state program, Marsha Kelley, also learned a great deal from the CHESP effort and developed the knowledge and skills to become one of the national leaders in the service-learning movement. The impact of the joint development, between the three components of the CHESP program with the collaboration and support of the state organization, made the impact of the entire project both transformational and of the highest quality. Mississippi, under Marsha and Tom's guidance, was considered one of the exemplary programs in the country and was looked upon as a shining example of what could be done when all sectors worked together.

In addition, the work of these individuals helped to spur the creation and implementation of a regional conference, the Gulf Summit, which continues through today as one of the finer efforts to maintain and improve inter-state collaboration and learning. Thus, the outcomes of the effort produced the kind of program quality and quantity necessary to maintain a full service-learning/civic engagement movement. And with Mississippi being one of the poorest states in the country, it has helped to mobilize the kind of talent and resources to address real issues of social injustice and the impacts of economic challenge.

DISCUSSION

The reason these two actions/activities were cited as examples of the best of the service-learning movement is because they embody the essential elements of impactful, sustainable, educational change. Three major elements are necessary for making efforts sustainable and high quality. I call them the 3Ms of long-term change in social institutions. They are mass, momentum, and money. Mass refers to an effort that continuously builds more and more programs and participants as the effort moves from year to year. Momentum refers to the speed at which the mass begins to move ... creating a force that expands each year, engaging more and more individuals and organizations in the process. And clearly money refers to the accumulation of financial resources to first begin the effort and then to sustain the program and projects for a long time to come. In both instances cited, the meeting in Washington, DC and the CHESP effort in Mississippi, a small effort expanded to include more people and groups so the impact and outcomes continued to grow, increase, and improve.

THE WORST OF TIMES

If these activities were considered the best of times for service-learning, then it should come as no surprise that I consider the worst of times for the field is when the Corporation for National and Community Service stopped funding for service-learning. This occurred in 2011 when funding for Learn and Serve America was eliminated in the House Appropriations Committee. Service-learning support ceased and thereafter CNCS primarily funded only efforts to support national service efforts, such as AmeriCorps, Senior Corps, and other adult projects. I think of this as one of the worst times because it meant the relative end of political and financial support for the service-learning field. The CNCS money had been used to fund state coordinators in all the states to assist collaboration among and between schools, colleges, and community organizations to develop service efforts that included academic learning and actual credit bearing experiences for students and young people at all levels.

So, it wasn't just about the loss of money and political support, it was also more a loss of the ability for the field to have a coordinating body that would seek to connect people and programs. Higher education was not quite as badly hurt by this action because Campus Compact had state coordinators in more than 30 states providing some level of coordination for colleges and universities. But, the ability and focus of connecting all levels took a step backward, and the field has suffered ever since.

Perhaps one of the most notable areas of decline has been attendance at the national service-learning conference, sponsored every year by the National Youth Leadership Council and Youth Service America. Attendance had been well over 2,000 for many of the years prior, with the CNCS funds helping many young people and adults across the country to attend. After the loss of funding, attendance has dropped to levels closer to 1,000, so the possibility for young people to attend and share with others across the country has been diminished.

The loss of funding also highlights a very important element of any education or social movement...the need for political support. The original legislation creating the National Service Act of 1990, the sponsoring legislation for the Corporation for National Service and later Corporation for National and Community Service, was born from efforts to connect members of both political parties, Democrats and Republicans, to ensure a strong foundation for long-term support. The loss of political and national support for service-learning was a most critical issue because the history of service-learning like programs, from the Progressive Era in the 1930s to the Career-Technical Education movement of the 1970s, all ended with political shifts that focused more on classroom-based instruction and away from community connected programming. Political directions spawned by reports, such as the Nation at Risk in the 1980s and the No Child Left Behind Act of the 2000s, set in motion the demise of service and community/student centered learning. This will become an important point to consider as we contemplate the future for service-learning and community/civic engagement.

SO, WHERE'S THE WISDOM?

If this is a brief description of the best and worst times in the service-learning movement, what can we learn from these events/trends that will help guide us to a more successful future for the field and for the movement. Well, from my perspective, it seems some very critical elements are clearly laid out. We need to learn from the past and imagine a future that ensures we mobilize our strengths and address the past actions that have led to the current loss of momentum and support.

First, we need to acknowledge that political winds have repeatedly blown the service-learning/student-centered schools/community-based experiential learning movements off course. In order to address these problems we need to act smarter and more effectively to ensure support and growth. This doesn't mean we need to act in a more partisan manner; in fact, quite the opposite. We need to remember that the goal of service-learning is civic engagement, helping people to understand their role, the issues, and the need for action in any democratic society. We need to have students, as they participate in their service-learning projects, to ensure that they have maximum visibility in the community to show what they are doing and the commensurate evaluation studies/data to show that what they are doing is making a difference. They need to demonstrate student learning, student engagement, community impact, and personal and community change. And they need to share it in a public view and engage with legislators and other policy people to understand how and why the service experiences are worthy of support and expansion. The ultimate goal of learning in a democracy is to prepare young people to become active, engaged citizens who use the principles of good experiential learning to make decisions and learn about the real issues in society.

Along this line, we need to encourage our youth, young adults, and adults who have participated in programs to actually walk the talk of civic engagement. They need to work with community advisory groups, local city councils, municipal and state governments, and even the federal government to educate policymakers about the value and impact of service-learning on individuals and communities. They need to take the lead to actually run for office to become public officials who can change and implement policy. For example, in Minnesota Paula Beugen has been a long time champion for service-learning and has worked with legislators to develop service-learning legislation on both the state and federal level. She also served as a member of a local school district board of education to ensure that appropriate policies were introduced around service-learning. Similarly, Jim Kielsmeier of the National Youth Leadership Council has worked with local, state, and federal officials to educate them about the strengths of service-learning and to assist in actually writing legislation that has led to the enactment of state and federal laws supporting service-learning. And Professor Joe Erickson of Augsburg College has worked to create a strong teacher education program while, and at the same time, actually running for membership on the Minneapolis Public Schools Board of Education, eventually becoming the chair of the board. These were the ones who understood the necessity of becoming an engaged citizen to ensure there were people creating policies and laws that clearly understood the importance of service-learning to the world of educational practice.

Even John Dewey, often considered the father of experiential learning and an advocate for student-centered, community-connected learning got involved in political issues. He worked to reduce concentrations of wealth in society for the few and sought to help the average person. In 1946, Dewey even attempted to help labor leaders establish a new political party, the People's Party, for the 1948 presidential elections.

Second, we need to heed the advice of those who have studied educational reform and put into practice those principles that are necessary for long-term growth and expansion. As highlighted in Seymour Sarason's (1990) *The Predictable Failure of Educational Reform,* any effort must include systemic change, where support comes from a variety of important social institutions. Tim Mazzoni, from the University of Minnesota, outlined what needed to occur for change to develop and thrive. Including at least four elements, teachers/administrators, parents, media, and legislators, in the process is critical to ensuring that all the members of society who wield power and influence are working to support the movement's growth, expansion, and sustainability.

The critical action in this process is empowering and mobilizing all those who can affect the movement. This means developing the capacity among organizations, institutions, and groups to all move in the same direction to help the efforts in schools, communities, and universities so that each can support the other and provide the necessary knowledge, skills, and processes to model what the movement is about. Professional development needs to be rooted in universities and schools of education, those groups charged with credentialing and training teachers. While the current movement has been blessed to have small organizations such as Youth Service America, the National Youth Leadership Council, the Constitutional Rights Foundation, and the Community Works Institutes providing training and staff development, they only reach a small portion of the teachers and faculty who need to be involved in a massive change of educational practice and purpose. They also need to connect to large national organizations that lead educational and community movements, such as the Association for Supervision and Curriculum Development (ASCD), the National Council for the Social Studies (NCSS), the National Dropout Prevention Network, the American Association for Colleges of Teacher Education, the American Educational Research Association, the American Association of Colleges and Universities, the Campus Compact, and the Community-Campus Partnerships for Health. The involvement of these large, systemic groups will help to create the capacity of the schools and universities of the nation to meet the challenges of preparing faculty, teachers, administrators, and staff in doing the work of service-learning.

Third, the strength of the service-learning has been always rooted in its own community, students. Students have been active in the movement as both the primary participants, but also as activists and promoters of the concept. From Wayne Meisel and Bobby Hackett, who helped start the Campus Outreach Opportunity League, to Craig and Marc Kielburger, who helped start the Free the Children program, young people have been actively involved in sharing their service, learning, and energy with projects and with the world. Their vitality and contributions, such as the Youth-Led Service-Learning Centers in Pennsylvania, have helped to serve the service-learning community, itself, by providing training for teachers, community members, and other students.

This involvement has set the tone and model for young people assuming leadership roles in building the capacity to expand service-learning across the United States and across the world. Young people can become the foundation for the future, working to ensure that service-learning is brought to their communities and to their lives. Youth can and should be the most important part of the future of service-learning, for they will be here during the next 40 years while many of us who have carried the movement for the past 40 years, will not. It is important for the service-learning movement to ensure that young people become the primary transmitters of the policies and practices in schools, in colleges, and in society. If there is to be a future for service-learning, it must be based on young people carrying the message for the next decades to come.

CONCLUSION

For more than 40 years, service-learning has been practiced, processed, and developed as an educational strategy to engage young people in the United States and around the world in active civic actions that lead to improved conditions in society and improved/increased learning on the part of participants. It's been done at the elementary, secondary, collegiate, and community levels, often with programs working with or between various sectors creating opportunities for community and personal change. It has been about making a difference in the lives of all involved.

Service-learning is not a new idea (Confucius had outlined some of its elements a few thousand years ago). It has been initiated, developed, and assessed for many years... and shown to have impact on all involved in the process. It is has blossomed and lingered over the many decades, achieving moments of heightened success and times of decline and reorganization. Throughout this period of history it has enjoyed the best of times and the worst... with the worst being far better than when it just was gathering steam and momentum in the 1960s and 1970s.

As recounted in this narrative, it has enjoyed moments where the concept of service-learning was being spread and shared with numerous organizations and institutions. It developed a strong following... and still has a good foundation for continued growth and engagement. But, it has also seen some recent declines in funding and support at the state and national levels in the United States and is in the process of reassessment and re-energizing its base. There is every reason to believe that the movement to engage young people in project-based learning, in community connected/

real-world programs that involve them in civic actions that promote and enhance academic, service, and practical learning will continue and thrive.

Service-learning will hopefully embody the three important elements of intellectual development espoused by Robert Sternberg (2003), educational psychologist. He has suggested there are three forms of intelligence: analytical, creative, and practical. This advice to educators is that they change the focus of education, to teach for wisdom, not knowledge. Hopefully, service-learning will provide the opportunities to connect all three, to apply analysis in creative ways that add an additional dimension... contribution to the improvement of society and the ability of individuals to work for a better world. That should be a great opportunity to take education and civil society to a heightened state... and to connect schooling, learning, and citizenship so that all may benefit from the actions of society.

REFERENCES

Rifkin, J. (1995). *The end of work: The decline of the global labor force and the dawn of the post-market era.* New York, NY: Putnam.

Saracen, S. (1990). *The predictable failure of educational reform.* San Francisco, CA: Jossey-Bass Publishers, Inc.

Sternberg, R. (2003). What is an "Expert Student?" *Educational Researcher, 32*(8), 5–9.

CHAPTER 10

SERVICE LEARNING

A Journey of a Lifetime

Cathryn Berger Kaye

HIGHPOINT: SERVICE LEARNING AS ADVENTURE[1]

I stumbled into service learning. As a first year teacher I was clueless about how to bring a classroom to life, let alone what to do when the kids showed up. Plus, my environment was unique. I was in the middle of Maine, teaching at the Sandy River School up a dirt road on Blueberry Hill in the town of Temple. We had three teachers, 22 kids age 6–17, a furnace I had to stoke in the frigid winter, and an outhouse.

The founders of the school were Mabel and George Dennison. Mabel was an extraordinary educator with the greatest understanding of child development I ever witnessed. George wrote a book chronicling Mabel's teaching in New York City in the 1970s, one of the first books on progressive education called *The Lives of Children* (Dennison, 1999). These two people influenced me then, and the influence has carried through my service learning pedagogy today.

Mabel's mantra: "Stop with the lesson plans, listen to the children." George constantly asked, "Where's the chaos?" referencing the creative

Where's the Wisdom in Service-Learning?, pages 143–155
Copyright © 2017 by Information Age Publishing
All rights of reproduction in any form reserved.

chaos where the dynamics of learning reside. Me? I was perplexed. Until Dutch Elm disease came to the area.

The students were outraged. Their trees were diseased, and worse, dying. "What are we going to do?" As a transplanted city gal I had no idea about the difference between an oak and an elm, so I was mystified. Finally, the messages of Mabel and George seeped into my brain and I responded, "What do you want to do about this? What do we need to know? "And what ensued was the true dynamic of student-generated learning: questions, community contacts, planning, and then being part of the brigade to assess trees for the state department of agriculture in partnership with university students.

What had I done? Listened to the children and built from their interests, skills, and talents. My lesson plans were replaced with learning experiences, heightened through the current emphasis on tree studies with a purpose—not just to learn about biology, but to save trees. The student learning soared as connections were made, and I was racing to keep up with the knowledge and skills being developed. I understood that controlling students was useless and pointless. Once we found meaning and purpose to learning, the natural chaos of life enlivened the learning. Ever since the year in Maine, when I enter a classroom that is too quiet and reserved, I cringe. Where is the learning?

When writing *The Complete Guide to Service Learning* (Kaye, 2010), first published in 2006, this is the story I re-discovered as my true beginning in service learning. I had a history of family service growing up, and witnessed service in its most authentic ways with my grandmother who had tremendous influence on how I saw the world. Her actions communicated "we are in this together." Service became a thread that continues to weave a strong tapestry in my family with my husband and daughters.

Service learning instills a sense of adventure in all participants, a shared journey. When tucking my elder daughter Ariel, then age five, into bed, she looked up at me with her big brown eyes and said, "Mommy, when am I going to have adventures like you?" At every age we seek life's adventure. Later when reading Milan Kundera's novel *Identity* I read the line: "Adventure is a way to embrace the world." Service learning, an authentic purposeful journey to embrace the world.

HIGHPOINT: A PROFESSIONAL DISCOVERY

How do youth become leaders? When this question became a central part of my professional work in 1981 at the Constitutional Rights Foundation, I sat at my desk for one month trying to come up with an answer. I had been tasked with developing a youth leadership program for high school students from Los Angeles and Orange counties. Unfortunately, I was making little progress until one beautiful day an echo from the past appeared: Listen to the children. I made appointments with every pair of students selected for this program from the 20 high schools and asked them what was important and mattered to them as young emerging leaders. The program appeared from their ideas and words, their queries and aspirations. And along with this came service. A leader, I decided, has to be doing something of value, taking action that benefits others while engaging others in the process. The program revolved quite successfully around service, with each student aiming to involve at least ten additional students in a worthwhile endeavor related to meeting an authenticated school or community need. This became Youth Leadership in Action.

The buzz about this program attracted the Ford Foundation to expand this effort within the Los Angeles Unified School District. In 1984, Youth Community Service was the largest and most extensive student service program within a school district, building the capacity of youth to come to know their communities and create meaningful service partnerships. Around 1987, a math teacher in the program piloted a service learning course at her high school and this made a shift into explicit academic connections, an established service learning process within a core class.

During this time, federal funding and interest built a momentum. How to spread the idea of service learning and youth engaged in service? The Constitutional Rights Foundation partnered with the Chief State School Officers Association to deliver three ground-shifting symposiums—Baltimore, Minneapolis, Los Angeles. Each state was expected to send a delegation to learn about this "service learning" idea and the program resonated well for all attendees (almost all—the delegation from Texas thought they were attending a seminar on "youth services" and immediately left).

With this growing interest, the first national newsletter about service learning, Constitutional Rights Foundation's School Youth Service Network hit the wires, and as editor for this unique publication I was continually connecting with educators finding their way to integrate service learning. Contributions came from across the country—articles sent by the speed of fax, in those days. Suddenly, educators and organizations were connected with exemplars and resources.

Had I discovered service learning or had it discovered me? Most definitely, I contributed to the discussion, conceptual ideas, and frameworks of what we know as service learning over the decades, however, this grew well beyond any group of people. Service learning became a national phenomenon that emerged. A handful of K–12 educators were there in the initial evolution; however, more joined the party, quickly. And of course service learning evolved outside the United States with robust examples, programs, and initiatives that thrive today.

I recall the voices of people thinking service learning would be a passing fancy, a trend that would burn out. Instead, the concepts and best practices continue to extend beyond the boundaries of any one nation or any grade level. As I travel the globe today, service learning is everywhere. I believe service learning will be a lasting pedagogy that is part of what will improve our education system for good.

HIGHPOINT: AN IDEA BEFORE ITS TIME

StarServe was the brain child of Mike Love of the Beach Boys. Often confused with the TV show "Star Search," StarServe, based in Santa Monica, California, was intended to grow service learning as a household concept. With funding from Kraft General Foods Foundation, the idea was unique for the times. Create service learning materials to educate teachers, K–12, and send them free of charge to every school in the United States. Add a dose of celebrity involvement to make this idea seem especially fun and attractive to kids and teens, and be available to answer questions through a toll-free 800 call-in number. Leading this program was an outstanding thinker, community organizer, and program developer, Gail Kong, from New York City, who is accomplished in social services and youth development. She asked me to join her in this endeavor and I was thrilled to join the party. We had funding for three exciting years.

The education packet, in English and Spanish, had versions for elementary and secondary levels. A colorful poster unfolded to show popular athletes, musicians, and actors who all support this idea of youth involved in service. We had several capable people at the ready to answer questions by phone, gather service learning stories, and send certificates to recognize the contributions of young people. I recall we fielded 40,000 calls in these three years. Additionally, we hosted service fairs in several cities to bring together youth and these artists to join in service together—meant to model service learning engagement and gain the publicity that would increase viability and knowledge of the strength of service learning for young people and the community. And we did an in-depth study of service learning in three schools, all aiming to use service learning as part of school reform: Washington State, Chicago, and Alvin, Texas.

StarServe traversed unfamiliar ground. To this day, I am unfortunately not convinced our distribution center did their job of distribution properly. Some in the field were uncertain about the celebrity participation; in those days this was not the norm. Celebrity endorsements? Now these are sought after. But then it made some service learning diehards skeptical of the validity of the program. I simply believe this was a concept before its time.

To this day, I still meet educators who say, "I got my start with StarServe." I know this program was remarkable in content and vision. Perhaps it is a footnote in the history of service learning in the United States, one that seeded service learning in more places and with more people than you might imagine.

ON MY OWN: A WORLD OF SERVICE LEARNING

After a summer assisting with the beginning of AmeriCorps in 1993, I became an independent consultant and writer about service learning. Returning to my initial quest for adventure, these years have been just that. After initially supporting schools, universities, organizations, agencies, districts, tribal nations, and states to advance service learning within the United States, I have had extensive opportunities to travel around the world to participate in the growth of high quality service learning.

In the United States, service learning was supported by federal funding and state offices that provided professional development and support. I was thrilled to consult with many states as service learning reached into rural, suburban, and urban America, both in K–12 settings and higher ed. Two places deserve mention, though there are many more.

Florida's Learn and Serve program extended deeply in education systems throughout the state. Their conferences and publications captured the vitality of service learning. They also partnered with Florida Campus Compact to provide a strong K–16 movement and integration.

Albion Central Schools, in Albion, New York, situated upstate between Buffalo and Rochester, made service learning a mainstay of the school system. This was a vision come true—service learning integration to contribute to a thriving community and equip young people with the skills, knowledge, and dispositions to be contributing members of society.

Consulting in these locales and elsewhere gave me a path for service learning growth as well, resulting in my writing *The Complete Guide to Service Learning: A Proven Practical...* in 2004, (a second edition arrived in 2010). Like most worthwhile endeavors, this took a village, and from my colleagues who provided examples of service learning stories, to my publisher, Free Spirit Publishing, who guided in numerous ways, this book continues to assist educators worldwide, now also published in Chinese by The Commercial Press (2016).

Extending my consulting outside the United States made it completely vivid that service learning is global and has been for decades. From Spain to Argentina, from Hong Kong and to Croatia, service learning is part of the vernacular, though there are differences in translation.

Governments and organizations want to support the concept of service learning in many parts of the world. Education systems contribute to growth, for example, the International Baccalaureate Programme has embraced quality service learning and has the ability to extend the concept globally.

LOOKING FORWARD: WILL SERVICE-LEARNING CRASH AND BURN IN AMERICA? NOT A CHANCE

Okay, it might. However, I don't believe that is possible.

Funding for Learn and Serve ended abruptly from my perspective. Too many states, school districts, and institutions for higher education that had not successfully embedded service learning as a best practice disappeared, some quickly, some slowly. Some reverted back to community service. Thankfully, many programs stayed in place or are growing anew.

As a teaching practice, service learning actually does not require huge amounts of dollars when embedded as a valued pedagogy. However, as a growing pedagogy still absent from most colleges of education and invisible in many school districts altogether, funding for professional development is essential. On the state level, having a service learning coordinator kept the topic visible and articulated, and ideally led to collaborating with other divisions. The sudden absence of funding was stunning. A community of educators mourned and questioned what would survive and whether service learning would vanish altogether.

Still going and still growing strong, service learning as a teaching and learning pedagogy deserves its place in education because service learning is great for schools and communities, and guides students to contribute to society so we can all build a thriving future.

What are lessons learned that will form effective guideposts for service learning's next generation of leaders? The following information sets the stage for future action.

GUIDEPOSTS FOR THIS NEXT GENERATION

1. *The Vision and the Will.* "Good" enough isn't. I have been in some of the "top" schools in the world striving to improve, seeing service learning as the missing link to more engaged and purposeful learning. Someone must see this—ideally some ones (that's plural), so there is momentum. When visiting the American International School of Johannesburg, these words from the school head, Andy Paige-Smith, resonated deeply about what provides the impetus: "You don't have to have all the answers. We listened to those who had passion and let this generate into something practical and worth being built upon. Administrators help clarify and make connections. We were willing to dream and follow our mission statement." When educators wait until all is known before taking the first step, the first step may never happen. Model risk taking to initiate service learning.

2. *Integrated, Integrated, Integrated.* Service learning is meant to improve the education process. When a teacher states, "I did service learning and didn't have to change much in my classroom," I have my doubts. Service learning changes how we approach content and how we engage youth, so they have voice and choice. Service learning moves the curriculum forward. Of course, service learning has viability in after school programs and clubs, youth councils, and organizations. All? Yes! However, in the purest form, service learning provides the reason for learning, to *apply* academic content—combines with prior knowledge and skills—to an authenticated issue in the community (more on "community" later). I have heard teachers exclaim, "How could I really teach without service learning?" Also, we know how the brain works. The brain seeks connectivity, and service learning is a naturally transdisciplinary construct that thrives on connections. Like our brains. Increase service learning = increase retention (among a myriad other benefits).

3. *Stakeholder Buy-In.* Leadership matters with any meaningful initiative. When an administrator allows time and resources for faculty to explore and learn about service learning methodologies, this provides a clear message. When the academic deans or curriculum coordinators understand their extremely vital role to ensure service learning is integrated into the curriculum and not an "add-on," again, this adds credibility to service learning as a valued pedagogy. When service learning is considered along with advancing other school priorities, this elevates its importance. For example, if a school priority is to improve inquiry or writing or school climate, take the time to recognize the role service learning can play in advancing this process by engaging teachers and students as partners. Professional development is also a necessary element, provided by the administration over the several years it will likely take for school-wide integration; then a path is set for this worthwhile journey.

   Listen to all the stakeholders. This can be the students, teachers, parents, administrators, support staff, community partners, higher education partners. Bringing collaborators to the table establishes collective ownership. Central to this approach is ensuring that all stakeholders have a clear understanding of what service learning is and how this teaching pedagogy transforms education.

4. *Know the Terms.* Language is the greatest communicator of culture. For a school or university to grow a culture of service learning, clarification of the words used is essential. Key words to explore include: volunteer, community service, service, community-based learning, projects, inquiry-based learning, design thinking, and, of

course, service learning. Find the similarities and differences. Expect conversations about "why call this service learning—does the term matter?" Actually, this should really just be called "excellent teaching" or "outstanding education." Until the process is embedded and understood by educators and policy makers, we need the language "service learning" that holds the idea and the ideal. And for all the terms and shiny new programs and approaches out there, I remain steadfast that service learning is the best. I have seen many "new" programs take the language of service learning and repackage or co-opt the concepts and with good reason—they work. Service learning is proven, reliable, and relatable. And you notice, in this chapter, service learning is without the "hyphen." I have been a hold out, along with others, and will not use the "–" for several reasons. I am not convinced it is grammatically correct or necessary, and it can read "minus!" If there were to be any symbol between the two, I would have this be the term "service + learning."

5. *Youth Voice and Choice.* Youth voice is not enough. That's just talk. Voice and *choice* means words transform into ideas and ideas into action. This will always be a challenge for educators, from pre-k through university. This changes the core paradigm of the "sage on the stage" or the central figure as the teacher who plans and arranges all. Control. That's what is challenged by service learning done well. How much classroom effort goes into control and management of students? Consider: Did you want to be controlled or managed when you were in school? Do you imagine today's students want to be "controlled and managed"? Admitting that many (if not most) educators are "control freaks," allows the beginning of recovery! By changing *control and manage* to *engage and inspire*, students have the wherewithal to discover their voice and their choice in the *learning* process. When extending the learning toward *service*, students discover a way to apply their learning to meet authenticated community needs.

6. *Recognize that Kids Already Make a Difference.* A common phrase students often hear in support of service learning is some form of "You can make a difference." According to environmental advocate Philippe Cousteau, kids cannot "make a difference." He continues by saying, "Kids already make a difference with every choice they make." All day long youth make a difference by whether they discard litter on the way home from school or purchase a single-use water bottle instead of using a refillable bottle. Consider the consumer power of youth and what their harnessed efforts could accomplish aimed at helping protect and preserve our environment. Of course, through service learning students can make significant contributions as they harness their interests, skills, talents, and knowledge and ap-

ply them to identified and confirmed needs. They contribute to the social well-being. They self-identify as change makers.

7. *Be Transparent Regarding the Five Stages of Service Learning.* At the moment of writing this article I hold that the five stages of service learning remain the most reliable construct for the service learning process" investigation, preparation, action, reflection, and demonstration. When students understand and can identify the five stages, and this can begin in primary grades, a common transferable language of learning has been established. Metacognition calls for this transparency and increases and provokes learning about learning. Also, students then learn a process they can apply to many aspects of their life, well beyond their academic years, as they continue to participate in social change.

**THE FIVE STAGES OF SERVICE LEARNING:
AN ABBREVIATED GUIDE**

Investigation: Includes the *inventory* of student interest, skills, and talents, and *social analysis* and verification of an identified need often through action research that includes use of media, interviews of experts, survey of varied populations, and direct observation/personal experiences.

Preparation: Students continue to acquire content *knowledge* as they deepen understanding, identify partners, *organize a plan of action,* clarify roles, build time lines, and continue developing *skills.*

Action: Students implement their plan in the form of *direct service, indirect service, advocacy,* or *research.* Action is planned with partners based on mutual understandings and perspectives.

Reflection: Reflection is *ongoing* and occurs as a considered *summation* of thoughts and feelings regarding essential questions and varied experiences to inform content knowledge, increase self-awareness, and assist in ongoing planning.

Demonstration: Students *capture the total experience,* including what has been learned, the process of the learning, and the service or contribution accomplished and shared with an audience; telling their story often integrates technology and further educates and informs others.

© 2014 CBK Associates.com

8. *Raise Questions.* One key purpose for service learning is to engender questions. This goes well beyond the first question that comes to mind. The intention is for students to discover the question beneath the original question, and the question below that one. The purpose is for depth of understanding. For example, if the original question is regarding *"How much food is needed by the local food bank?"* the sub-question *below* this one may be *"What circumstances cause poverty in our community?"* Questions can continue to take the inquiry deeper and deeper to include systemic considerations and ethical dilemmas. The point is to refuse to be satisfied by the obvious. This may disturb the status quo. Questions can also cause a purposeful disturbance as the vantage point can move from local to global issues, since what occurs in one place is connected to what occurs somewhere else. This, then, can provoke another critical question: Do students need to travel to distant places when they can find relevant and essential and often similar issues to those in their own backyard? What creates the greatest opportunity for meaningful service and significant ongoing relationships?

9. *What is the Service, Really?* Putting up posters about an issue as "advocacy service," to teach others in your school about the issue, is not service learning unless this is confirmed as an articulated need. Most likely it is a quick "let's get the service in service learning done" way to tick off the box. Sometimes, the idea of service is thought of too little and too late to do something of value. If service is an afterthought, the outcome will be scant. While some think this should be called "learning service," I completely disagree. The term "service learning" is correct. Service has to be in the mind of all involved as we set out on the course of learning so we have direction. This is different from having a goal—This is setting a course. A goal can be overly prescriptive and reduces the capacity for thinking in the moment and participating in the winding journey of learning. Fixation on a goal can reduce possibility and potential and lock into a preset mindset. Plus, to actually have youth voice and choice we have to head into the unknown. As we move through learning, "service" aligns purpose to process. If, instead, we get to the end of the learning and think, "Now, what can be the service?" we have missed the proverbial boat. Now, with those posters in the school, this can be a beta, a tester, to determine which posters would be most effective in the community. Tutoring younger children in your school is practice for teaching them in a community center or other locale where this is highly needed.

We must up the ante on service, so I present another lens to look at this construct. Consider that service can be:

- Kind—sitting with an elder person to give them company
- Helpful—leading conversations with elders on current events to stimulate mental acuity
- Compassionate—responsive to an urgent crises or disaster
- Disruptive—shifting the status quo so we move forward as a society

10. *Aim for Reciprocity.* Service learning always aims for reciprocity, a mutual exchange with benefits for all involved. This becomes a centerpiece for service learning and is achieved through ongoing dialogue with all partners. With an understanding of the term *reciprocity* and awareness that service learning is done with others, this removes the onus that service learning further delineates the "haves" and the "have-nots." Instead, this establishes the recognition that all participants have value and all contribute to the learning and the service. For example, when high school students visited a shelter—a residential facility for unemployed men— the residents were all out for the day seeking employment. The students noticed an extensive library and asked why there were so many books. The program director explained that the men tire of watching television and instead spend many nights reading. A student asked if they could start a book club with residents who would be willing to participate. The young male students scheduled monthly discussions about mutually agreed upon books with eager self-selected participants living at the shelter. With this example, it is difficult to say who benefited the most. Keep reciprocity in mind. Discuss the term, and be on the lookout for those significant moments when reciprocity becomes tangible. The educator's role is to be more attentive to this relationship and may find that when following the five stages of service learning, reciprocity is more likely.

11. *Reexamine Reflection.* The purpose of reflection is not to reflect; it is to become reflective. This means that rote prompts and counting how many "reflections" are turned in will not be effective in developing this natural instinctive habit of mind. Consider all the ways a person can enter reflection, including your preferred ways. How can students experience a range of entry points to experience reflection *by choice*? This is fertile ground for exploration and discovery, and essential in the service learning process. When students are guided to be on the lookout for significant moments in the learning and in the service they will likely be responsive

with what matters most. When students have an array of ways to be expressive they will select the most meaningful way to express themselves. Educators can facilitate reflection as a purposeful self-determined act of heart and mind.

12. *Grow a Community.* Be part of a local, regional, national, and international community of practitioners who get the power, the purpose, and the process of service learning. Gain the perspective needed from others in completely different circumstances. They open our eyes. Listen. Travel. See. Be on the lookout for those who would want to be change agents and would benefit from service learning knowledge, and be a co-collaborator. Service learning by its very design brings people together. Any dozen needs one more, a "baker's dozen."

13. *Capture the Stories.* This is so important. We will forever need the stories of what happened through service learning—and *please* not just the "service." We need the story of the +. What happened because these two elements were put together. Capture all the elements of the five stages, each one, even those that appear routine, like taking a photo of students having a conversation. When we only later show others the service, they can rightfully question, "Why is this happening in schools? Where is the learning?" Show it all. Capture the entire process so service + learning is vivid, compelling, real, and significant.

Service learning has changed many lives, including mine. Through what feels to be a century-long journey, I have seen the world with new ideas, and been transformed by people through their stories and their dedication to community. I am encouraged by younger generations who know that we face astounding challenges and see service learning as a process that will be viable for the children they will nurture into stewards for our collective future.

Cathryn Berger Kaye, M.A., CBK Associates, is an international education consultant and the author of *The Complete Guide to Service Learning* plus two books with environmental advocate Philippe Cousteau, *Going Blue* and *Make a Splash!* For additional articles visit www.cbkassociates.com and to reach Cathryn, email cathy@cbkassociates.com.

NOTE

1. Portions/ideas contained in this chapter appear in other publications by Cathy Berger Kaye, and can be found at http://www.cbkassociates.com/resources

REFERENCES

Dennison, G. (1999). *The lives of children: The story of the First Street School.* Portsmouth, NH: Heinemann Educational Books.

Kaye, C. B. (2010). *The complete guide to service learning.* Minneapolis, MN: Free Spirit.

CHAPTER 11

THE WISDOM OF BOBBY HACKETT

Bobby Hackett

Like many people, my early experiences shaped much of what I've gone on to do in my career. In my case, I was exposed to a series of ideas in my first two jobs that I've been working through ever since. In the process I have often used the metaphor of constructing a building, one floor at a time. The core ideas have guided my approach to designing each floor and set my goals for how the final structure would be.

INSPIRING LEGACY

The first big idea—community-led change—I learned while interning with my father at the Youth Policy Institute, which I did off and on, since the 11th grade. I learned about his focus on supporting communities to fight poverty (and replaced challenges) through a process of organizing and implementing comprehensive, integrated plans at the local or neighborhood level.

My father had been at the center of President Kennedy's efforts to address the issue of poverty and juvenile delinquency. Working with the attorney general, Robert Kennedy, and his "Hackett's Guerrillas" he developed

Where's the Wisdom in Service-Learning?, pages 157–169
Copyright © 2017 by Information Age Publishing
All rights of reproduction in any form reserved.

what came to be the federal Community Action Program and VISTA (Volunteers in Service to America). Both of these War on Poverty programs were centerpieces of President Lyndon Johnson's Economic Opportunity Act of 1964. My father piloted these bottom-up community empowerment strategies in response to the poverty they had seen firsthand during the extended West Virginia primary in the 1960 presidential campaign.

After the president's victory, my father (all of 34 years old at the time!) was appointed executive director of the president's committee on Juvenile Delinquency and Youth Crime, which was established to address the rising gang problem facing many cities. Working out of an office next to Robert Kennedy's, my father met with experts on the different issue areas related to delinquency—education, labor, health, justice, housing—trying to find the best thinking at the time to address the issue. Eventually, he was convinced by the argument advocated by Lloyd Ohlin that delinquency was a symptom of the larger problem of poverty and that to attack poverty you needed to work holistically at the neighborhood level. The president's committee began by making planning grants in 16 cities, with the expectation that the communities would develop comprehensive, integrated plans that linked diverse ranges of organizations and programs that addressed distinct but related causes of poverty. About a year into their work they added a requirement that the residents of these low income communities had to have a seat at the table, adding their voice to the decision-making about what programs should get funded to meet the needs and opportunities in their communities. This became the "maximum feasible participation of the poor" language in the Community Action Program section of the Johnson anti-poverty bill.

While my father never shared war stories, he often spoke about this idea. Without the power of the presidency and federal funding, he was determined to build a database of model programs and policy options to empower communities with the best thinking on how to tackle the problems they faced. His goal was to help community groups avoid the problem of "reinventing the wheel" by providing them with lessons learned about what works and with information about funding opportunities.

My father set out to accomplish this through the Youth Policy Institute (YPI), a non-profit, nonpartisan research organization he started to inform citizens so that they can shape policies and programs which affect their neighborhoods and their lives. YPI believes that sound program strategies can emerge only from informed deliberation coupled with neighborhood participation. To support and spark that debate, the Institute published objective reports on current, past and proposed policies and programs.

The second formative idea that has guided my work—students as community-based researchers—grew out of my experience, first as a high school and later as a college student, interning at YPI. I remember in 1978 helping build the first bookshelves and drafting the first one-page issue brief (on testing for college entrance) that would highlight the scope of the problem, past policy milestones, current policy, brief profiles of distinctly different policy options, a listing of key organizations and individuals, followed by a glossary of terms. In the 1980s and through the mid-'90s, YPI published two monthly magazines and a journal, and initiated demonstration projects with neighborhood-based urban and rural coalitions to inform their planning processes. The research and publishing was conducted in YPI's offices in Washington, DC by college and recent graduate-aged analysts guided by a core staff of professionals.

Over the years, YPI employed more than 800 young people as staff and interns. What I learned from my experience working beside so many other students my age was that we were capable of doing serious work on serious issues. My father pushed us hard and had faith that we should and could attend congressional hearings, interview policy experts in and outside of government, and translate what we learned into practical analysis and useful facts that inspire and inform action in communities across the country.

BUILDING A MOVEMENT

The next stage of my education came during college when I got to know a student a few years ahead of me, Wayne Meisel, who had been active in organizing new community service programs. These included the first Cambridge Youth Soccer League and a partnership with the Saturday Special Needs Youth Program he brought to campus. After graduating, Wayne spent a year organizing the House and Neighborhood Development (HAND) project which formed one-to-one partnerships between the Harvard houses (essentially big dorms with their own dining halls and libraries) with the neighborhood schools surrounding campus. This project was further proof that students wanted to be engaged in the local community but needed structures (like HAND) and encouragement from other students like ourselves who were already active.

That experience gave Wayne the inspiration to launch a national organization to tap and channel the idealism of students to lead a service movement on their campuses, much as he had done at Harvard. In addition, Wayne had discovered (through research he conducted at my father's insistence during a several month internship at YPI) that at the turn of the 20th century there were 700 campus YMCAs whose primary purpose was service. The campus Ys had largely disappeared by the time we were in college in the early 1980s. Wayne wanted to revive that student service movement. With my father's help, he wrote a successful grant proposal from the Hazen Foundation in New York City and used the funding to return to a number of campuses during the fall of 1984 that he had come to know on an 800+ mile walk he had taken the previous winter and spring from Maine to Washington, DC to promote his cause.

Given my experience at YPI, it didn't take much to persuade me to spend the spring semester of my senior year organizing the first Campus Outreach Opportunity League (COOL) conference. We were able to recruit 125 students and staff to attend this meeting during Harvard's March 1985 spring break. Our keynote speaker was Dr. Robert Coles, a popular professor who often spoke about the civil rights movement and his own interest in change makers like Dorothy Day, Ruby Bridges, and other social justice-minded writers and poets.

With Dr. Coles' assistance, Wayne and I were awarded a two-year fellowship from the Lyndhurst Foundation that enabled us both to work on COOL full-time. Our initial goal was to disprove the popular belief that we were the "Me Generation." Our contention that young people wanted to serve, just as we had seen at college and as I had seen at the Youth Policy Institute. Given the lack of campus infrastructure for mobilizing student energy for community service, we had to start at the ground level, which meant recruiting and organizing students to volunteer.

For young people today it might be hard to imagine starting a national organization without the internet and the ability to broadcast your message at virtually no cost to anyone who would listen. Back then, our only real choice was to get on the road to meet students and faculty and staff. Therefore, I used my fellowship award to buy a red pickup truck (with a cab on the back and a futon inside for when I couldn't snag a dorm room couch to sleep on). We were on the road constantly, building relationships one campus at a time, holding our annual conference each spring break, publishing a newsletter with the desktop printing technology that had just arrived, and printing our first handbook, *Building a Movement: Students in Community Service.*

While our hands-on approach was slower then to get the word out than we would have today, one distinct advantage was that we knew firsthand what was happening on campuses all across the country. Our momentum built gradually at first, with 125 people attending each of our first two national conferences at Harvard and then Brown Universities. With our third conference at Georgetown University we nearly tripled attendance to 350 people. Two years later, COOL's fifth annual conference brought together 1,500 students and staff from all across the country under a new logo designed by Keith Haring.

In this process, I came to the next idea that has fueled my work: young people should be key leaders of a youth service movement. Just as my father was seeking to empower citizens of local neighborhoods with the information they need to lead their own community change process, I came to understand that students can be empowered to do the same on their campuses. That was COOL's mission in a nutshell. And, at the time, we were the only national organization in the youth service movement run for and by young people.

One of our biggest challenges was proving that recent college graduates could be trusted by funders to help lead this movement. We sometimes had people looking at us skeptically, asking as a Yale graduate school student did one night over dinner, "Who gave you permission to do this?" This attitude only fueled our ambition to change how people viewed the capacity of young people to lead change in higher education. Despite struggling to be taken seriously by some of the Foundations which were beginning to pour funding into the national service movement, COOL raised funding from the Kellogg Foundation and others to expand beyond our initial focus on co-curricular community service, including creating programs like Teaming Up that partnered students with faculty to create service-learning courses.

For all the excitement and promise of the early COOL days, I was nearing my 27th birthday and I understood that it was time to step down. I went to graduate school in management with the goal of learning how to lead a non-profit organization, having learned a lot in the last three years about what not to do.

COOL GOES TO A FOUNDATION

Soon after I went off to graduate school in management, Wayne Meisel was invited to become the founding president of the Corella and Bertram F. Bonner Foundation. Once there, Wayne worked with Mr. Bonner and the John Stephenson, president of Berea College, to pilot a service-based scholarship program beginning the the fall of 1990. Inspired in part by the work program at Berea, the Bonner scholarship was structured so that the work portion of a student's financial aid package would be met by off-campus community service work. Within two years, the Foundation had expanded the Bonner Scholars Program to 22 colleges, mostly in the Appalachian region.

Meanwhile, after graduate school I went to work at the Office of Management and Budget (OMB), where I got an inside look at policymaking at the highest level of the federal government. This experience confirmed my desire to work at the local level where I could see the impact of my actions.

So, I left OMB to work with an affordable housing developer, Marilyn Melkonian, who "believes that physical and community development are inseparable." Telesis Corporation's "work reflects and encompasses the values of civil engagement, education, health, housing, green living, cultural leadership, and democracy." Marilyn had been influenced, in part, by my father who shared her vision to "develop and manage comprehensive revitalization, from affordable home ownership opportunities to mixed-income rental opportunities; from world-class architecture to world-class landscape design; from learning centers to employment centers; from community policing to community daycare." In many ways, this was an ideal place for me to work on my first idea—supporting local residents in their efforts to combat poverty in their community. But, I also came to understand that Telesis was first and foremost a housing developer and my skills and aptitude were not suited to that side of the business. So while I could work through my first big idea, I wasn't able to work on the others—specifically mobilizing students to support community groups with the information and analysis to inform their change process.

With that in mind, I rejoined Wayne in the spring of 1992 when the Bonner Scholars Program was still just getting off the ground. What brought me back was the opportunity to pick-up where I had left off with COOL, trading the breadth of building a national organization supporting hundreds of campuses for the depth of a program supporting 1,500 students on 22 campuses who receive "access to education and an opportunity to serve."

The Bonner Foundation's financial support allows the participating schools to recruit and mobilize cohorts of 60 to 100 low-income students who then become leaders on their campuses and in their local communities. With this resource, I saw that I could work through my ideas for informing community change leaders at the local level through the efforts of talented and motivated college and university students.

From the very beginning I understood that the Bonner Scholars Program model would enable these students to lead campus change in three ways. First, these students would raise the bar for how campuses viewed student development through community engagement for the simple fact that they would receive consistent and increasing levels of training, reflection, and responsibility by serving 10 hours per week (plus 2 hours in summers) over 4 years. Before Bonner, no one in higher education had access to this much time to work with this many students in developing their skills, knowledge and interests in civic engagement, community building, social justice, diversity, spiritual exploration, and international perspective (the Bonner Common Commitments).

Second, through consistent engagement and increasing their skills and knowledge of community change, the Bonner Scholars would redefine how community partners directed college or university assets to support community-defined programs and change processes. In their 4 years in the program, students in the Bonner Program would move developmentally through phases of engagement beginning with exploring their service interests, focusing their energy on a primary service issue or organization, rising to higher levels of responsibility coordinating other student volunteers, then taking on capacity-building building projects using the training and education they receive in and outside their classrooms.

Finally, with encouragement from the foundation and their campus staff, Bonner Scholars would help lead the development of a campuswide culture for service, and take on positions that rebuilt the infrastructure to lead that community engagement. Beginning in the first years of the program, the community and intellectual commitments and engagements of these students was noticed by all they met, including by faculty who remarked on the real world perspective and connections they brought to their academic work and classroom discussions and by community partners who valued their tireless dedication to their organizations and neighborhoods.

I have been at the Bonner Foundation working for more than 25 years now, connected to a network of more than 60 colleges and universities supporting 3,000 students per year who serve and learn through their Bonner Program on the campuses. Our primary focus has been on building a culture of service on these campuses, and the infrastructure to support that culture so that, as we would say when we were at COOL, "everybody, everyday" is challenged and supported to serve.

Initially, we had to learn how best to structure each component of the Bonner Program operations, from recruitment and selection to financial aid packaging and what to include in the weekly Bonner training and reflection meetings. We had to wait until the fifth year when we had graduated the first class of Bonners before we could identify the stages of personal and intellectual development that characterize the Bonner model. Eventually, these were described as the five E's: Expectation, Exploration, Experience, Example, and Example. A few years later Ariane Hoy (then Executive Director of COOL) began developing an extensive series of training modules for schools that we continue to add to since she joined the Bonner Foundation staff in 2004.

At the same time we were developing the Bonner Program, we were also working with schools to establish campuswide centers that sought to organize and coordinate community and civic engagement that could involve every student, faculty, and staff member. Indeed, probably the most remarkable evolution in the service movement is that virtually every campus in the country now has a center or office devoted to this purpose. Experiential learning through service, internships, and course-based opportunities, is featured prominently in university websites and admissions packets. Indeed, the vital role of community and civic engagement has reached the highest levels of campus strategic priorities, due in part to the compelling research on student learning outcomes and calls to action put forth so convincingly in *A Crucible Moment: College Learning and Democracy's Future* (The National Task Force, 2012) by the Association of American Colleges & Universities, among other calls to action.

One quality of the culture developed in the Bonner Program that is worth mentioning is how students have come to define their commitment in relation to the ideal Martin Luther King referred to as "The Beloved Community." The intensity and depth of Bonner service in communities different from their own, the sheer joy of being with people different from themselves, began to be expressed as and motivated by "Bonner Love." This phrase has spread throughout our network as a way of articulating who they are and what they do. At a time when many campuses are searching for ways to bring people together across differences, the Bonners have shown how this might happen for others through consistent engagement in service, reinforced and amplified through structured and unstructured reflection in Bonner workshops, classes, long bus rides on service trips, and with their community partners.

COMMUNITY-DEFINED RESEARCH

When I returned to the Bonner Foundation, I also began trying different ways to incorporate community-based research into our programming. I added an exercise at our first major Summer Leadership Institute in May 1993 where we mapped the poverty, crime, and employment rates in Greensboro, North Carolina. While this was a useful first step, it was clear that we had a lot to learn if we were to introduce this kind of practical community research as an integral and feasible activity of our campuses.

In 1997, we were awarded our first of three Federal grants by the Learn & Serve America Program of the Corporation for National and Community Service with the goal of incorporating community-based research as a form of service learning into academic courses and internships. This came 20 years after I was first exposed to this approach by my father at the Youth Policy Institute and 5 years after I started at the Bonner Foundation.

Fortunately, we did not have to start from scratch. Community-based research (CBR but also known by several other labels, including participatory action research) had been practiced and written about by people such as John Gaventa, at the University of Tennessee, Knoxville, and Phil Nyden at Loyola University Chicago. With their writing as a starting point and the federal grant support, we were able to experiment with how to incorporate CBR as a form of service learning on a wide variety of campuses. The initial group of schools ranged from Middlesex County College in New Jersey, to Guilford College in North Carolina, to the University of Michigan, the University of Denver, and Princeton University.

Our nine years of Learn & Serve funding yielded many important insights and resources. For instance, we found that the principles and practices of community-based research were exactly the same regardless of the type of school we were working with. What differed was what it took to convince a community college, 4-year year liberal arts college, or research university to participate. We also learned that few community partners had the experience of requesting research assistance that would be of practical benefit to them, so extra effort has to be put into nurturing those relationships to develop and complete successful community-based research projects.

These and other lessons are found in a series of important publications that grew out of these grants, including what we fondly refer to as the "purple book" entitled *Community-Based Research and Higher Education: Principles and Practices* (Strand, Marullo, Cutforth, Stoecker, & Donohue, 2003) co-authored by five faculty in our original 1997 grant. Subsequently, Deanna Cooke from Georgetown University and Trisha Thorme from Princeton University published *A Practical Handbook for Supporting Community-Based Research with Undergraduate Students* (2011). And most recently Mary Beckman and Joyce Long from the University of Notre Dame published *Community-Based Research: Teaching for Community Impact* (2016) which includes many case studies from our third Learn & Serve CBR grant.

At one point we noticed that we weren't receiving the public policy oriented research requests that I had anticipated, especially inquiries about the most effective approaches or programs for addressing issues in the community. To generate public policy-oriented research questions, we used Learn and Serve funds to support faculty on 20 different campuses to identify community partners interested in public policy research questions. Students did research and published issue briefs on the PolicyOptions wiki using the template my father had developed at the Youth Policy Institute. The students presented their findings directly to local partners in public meetings, conferences, and other community-based settings. The community partners valued the profiles of model programs and the format of the issue briefs for synthesizing and presenting a range of information on each topic in an easily digestible form. Faculty liked this format because it forced students to examine a variety of solutions to a community problem and to put those solutions in the context of past and current efforts. Students found the template easy to follow, though we learned many students are initially uncomfortable picking up the phone or meeting with community or policy leaders face to face.

COMMUNITY-DRIVEN CHANGE

The modest but hard earned success of these community-based research projects set the stage for the fourth and perhaps most far reaching idea I've been working through: The notion that our campus community engagement strategies should be driven first and foremost by our commitment to community change.

A community-driven change agenda does not compromise our goals for student learning or sustaining higher education institutions. Instead, maintaining a clear focus on how students and campuses can most effectively contribute to community-defined change provides both the imperative and direction for how to go about designing our educational and institutional responses to the many challenges facing higher education today.

In the Bonner Transformation Goals, which we formalized a few years ago, we define a series of goals in concentric circles, with the innermost circle representing individuals and places, with each encompassing circle representing programs, organizations, and finally systems. What's unique perhaps is that for each level (or circle) our goals for campus and students are matched by our goals for organizations and communities. Our community-driven goals begin with directly supporting individuals and places (specifically places in terms of the natural and built environment). Surrounding that, we define our goals to help develop and manage evidence-based programs that mobilize students and others to provide that direct support. These first two levels are, in fact, the predominate form of student engagement on campuses across the country.

The two outer circles of our transformation goals are where I think we will make are most important contributions to community-defined change. We now need to organize our campuses so we can more effectively provide organizational capacity support to direct service-providing organizations (such as after school programs or soup kitchens) and at local collaboratives seeking to bring about change at a systemic level (such as local cradle to career coalitions or a local alliances to end homelessness).

This is a big difference from where most of the field is today. For as long as I've been active in this field we have described the arc of our work as moving from service to advocacy, from charity to justice. And yet, while everyone talks about the importance of meeting community needs, our practice has inevitably prioritized student and institutional outcomes. I am not alone in recognizing that we have a lot of work to do before we fully realize higher education's potential in educating and mobilizing students, staff, faculty, and higher education institutions themselves, to be effective allies and partners for the community groups and individuals working to bring about positive change in their communities.

I will close by sharing the three major tasks ahead of us if we are to to fully realize higher education's potential for preparing civic leaders and playing an active role in community problem solving.

First, we must expand our core community partnerships to include collaboratives and campaigns. In Figure 11.1 we simplify our community partners into three categories: service provider, collaboratives, and campaigns.

Partners	Service Provider		Collaborative	Campaign
Roles	Client Service	Program Coordinator	Organization Capacity Building	Advocacy
Tasks	e.g., tutoring, serving soup, etc.	Recruiting, training, and supervising volunteers	1) Volunteer Management 2) Program Development 3) Fundraising 4) Communication 5) Research: CBR & PolicyOptions	e.g., letter writing, community organizing, etc.
Program Structures	Clearinghouse/Directory Listing of Opportunities (online database)			
	Site/Issue-Based Teams (coalition of student-led service projects)			
	Bonner Program (four year training & increased roles culminating in capstone project)			
Academic Structures	Service-Learning & Community-Based Research Courses			
		Problem / Issue-Based Concentrations (courses, service roles, CBR, and capstone project)		
		Skill-based Certificate / Fellowships (courses, client-defined capacity-building projects)		

Figure 11.1 Community engagement models.

As you'll see, we have defined four ways students service is received from a community partner perspective: direct service, coordinating direct service, organizational capacity building, and advocacy. Figure 11.1 shows how organizational capacity building by students can occur with all three kinds of community-based organizations. Even after all these years, almost all community-campus partnerships are with service providing groups for students doing direct service and program coordination, while the vast majority of capacity building in the form of volunteer management and a modest amount of community-based research. In the interest of engaging students in policy research and other forms of community-problem solving, campuses need to reach out to the coalitions, alliances, government commissions, and other neighborhood-based, multi-agency collaboratives that were working at a systemic level to coordinate, collaborate, or take on collective impact approaches to addressing local needs and opportunities for change. We must also train students in social action, where they learn how to organize to effect policy change.

Second, we must create pathways for student and community partner engagement that are defined by the issues or problems we and our partners seek to solve, such as food security or community health. In addition, we should organize pathways defined by the skills or competencies for community engagement, such as policy research, non-profit management, and communication. These two approaches to creating community engagement pathways for students combine academic coursework, community-based research, and direct engagement opportunities culminating in community-engaged capstones or signature work projects. The progression from direct service placement to capacity-building project reflects the developmental pathway experienced by students in the Bonner Program. Both of the approaches prepare students to provide their highest level of project-based problem-solving support to community partners, and thus achieving our highest level of support for addressing the issues facing these organizations and the communities they serve.

Third, we need to create new infrastructure and staffing models for supporting this work. These include roles for faculty in developing and coaching student community-engagement projects, which will require, for instance, rethinking the credit hour (to escape the bonds of the traditional three or four credit semester course) and how we train, support, and recognize faculty work. To create the problem-based pathways described above, we will need new academic credit-bearing options that stand outside the traditional academic disciplinary lines. We will also need new centers or institutes to bring together the expertise on specific capacity-building project areas such as non-profit management, communication, and community policy research.

Fortunately, all of these ideas and more have already taken form on one campus or another. Our challenge now is to develop, expand on, and share these models in ways that build on the legacy of 40+ years of service learning and civic engagement while at the same time expanding its impact on communities, students, and the colleges and universities that bring them together.

REFERENCES

Beckman, M., & Long, J. F. (2016). *Community-based research: Teaching for community impact.* Sterling, VA: Stylus.

Cooke, D., & Thorme, T. (2011). *A practical handbook for supporting community-based research with undergraduate students.* Washington, DC: Council on Undergraduate Research.

Economic Opportunity Act of 1964, Pub. L. No. 88-452, 78 Stat. 508 (1964).

The National Task Force on Civic Learning and Democratic Engagement. (2012). *A crucible moment: College learning and democracy's future.* Washington, DC: Association of American Colleges and Universities. Retrieved from https://www.aacu.org/sites/default/files/files/crucible/Crucible_508F.pdf

Strand, K., Marullo, S., Cutforth, N., Stoecker, R., & Donohue, P. (2003). *Community-Based Research and Higher Education: Principles and Practices.* San Franciso, CA: Jossey-Bass.

ADDITIONAL READING

The Unraveling of America: A History of Liberalism in the 1960s by Allen J. Matusow.

Impossible Democracy: The Unlikely Success of the War on Poverty Community Action Programs by Noel A. Cazenave.

Scouting the War on Poverty: Social Reform Politics in the Kennedy Administration by Daniel Knapp and Kenneth Polk.

Poverty Knowledge: Social Science, Social Policy, and the Poor in Twentieth-Century U.S. History by Alice O'Connor.

President of the Other America: Robert Kennedy & the Politics of Poverty by Edward R. Schmitt.

Mobilization and Poverty Law: Searching for Participatory Democracy Amid the Ashes of the War on Poverty by Wendy A. Bach.

Community-Based Research and Higher Education Principles and Practices by Kerry Strand, Sam Marullo, Nick Cutforth, Randy Stoecker, and Patrick Donohue. San Francisco, CA: Jossey-Bass 2003. "Guide to incorporating a new form of scholarship into academic settings. Presents a model of community-based research that engages community members with students and faculty in the course of their academic work."

Community-Based Research: Teaching for Community Impact by Mary Beckman (Editor), Joyce F. Long (Editor), Timothy K. Eatman (Foreword).

Liberating Service Learning and the Rest of Higher Education Civic Engagement by Randy Stoecker.

A Practical Handbook for Supporting Community-Based Research with Undergraduate Students by Trisha Thorme and Deanne Cooke.

CHAPTER 12

FROM A CHANCE TO THE DANCE, OR FROM HAPPENSTANCE TO HAPPENING

Robert Shumer

The previous stories, from 95-year-old John Duley to 55-year-old younger-ster Bobby Hackett, tell tales of how people got involved in service-learning efforts and what they did along the way to promote the field. The stories are fascinating and provide a multitude of examples of different entry points and different paths to today's world. They are filled with great examples of how people evolved over time and how they worked, connected, and grew personally as they developed a field.

Common to their stories are two major themes. No one started out doing service learning. Not as a professional. Not as a lay person. But they all had an event, an opportunity, an experience that heightened their awareness of the principles of service learning and allowed them to take actions and do things that have had enormous repurcussions for the field. Thus, every-one started with a chance occurrence. And everyone made things happen through personal initiative and through networks and collaborations. I call

Where's the Wisdom in Service-Learning?, pages 171–178
Copyright © 2017 by Information Age Publishing
All rights of reproduction in any form reserved.

these themes "from chance to the dance and from happenstance to happening." Everyone started with an unplanned, chance beginning. Everyone took that opportunity to make something happen in their world and the world around them.

This theme was aptly described by Bill Ramsay in his chapter. He related the story of a Princeton professor who discussed "the lucky accident and the prepared mind." Repeated here, it frames the contructs of happenstance to happening and suggests that such "discoveries" have been around for a long time.

> In my Oak Ridge years I heard a lecture by Dr. Hubert Alyea, a Princeton professor of chemistry, which he entitled "The Lucky Accident and the Prepared Mind." His thesis was that many important scientific discoveries were made when a "prepared mind" saw something that happened by accident and related it to other knowledge in a new way. He cited Newton seeing an apple fall and "discovering" gravity; Marie and Pierre Curie's discovery of radiation; a DuPont chemist, Roy Plunket discovering "Teflon." None of these advances in science were the result of carefully designed experiments.

This same phenomenon was also reported in the Horatio Alger books of the 19th century. Alger wrote of "rags to riches" stories, of young impoverished children who rose to middle-class or wealthy status because of many attributes, including hard work, some act of bravery, and a mysterious stranger (who helps the young person to achieve success). The Horatio Alger "myth" often referred to the road to success as an occurance that included "pluck and luck." For Alger, the "prepared mind" was the hard work and preparation, and the "lucky accident" was the chance meeting of someone who would provide the connections that lead to success. So, the story of "chance to the dance and happenstance to happening" is not a new one.

So it is that all of our authors fit into this interesting process. John Duley begins his story with a description of his involvement in Michigan State's Rust College and the Civil Rights movement. It was happenstance that the civil rights efforts occurrend while he was Chaplin at MSU. And it was also chance that a student, Mary Ann Shupenko, who had participated in the Freedom Summer and was a close personal friend of Professor Robert Green, called to inform him of what was happening in Mississippi. As a result of that call, and ensuing actions by Green and Duley, the Student Tutorial Education Project began. The rest is history . . . of an incredible service-learning program between Michigan State and Rust College . . . and the lifelong engagement of John Duley in creating programs of social action.

William Ramsay tells us of the various chance occurences that led to his involvement at the Oak Ridge Institute of Nuclear Studies. Nuclear scientists were looking for positive uses of such energy after the devastation during World War II. They didn't have the equipment necessary to do further investigations, so they created internships through southern universities to pursue studies and programs that would provide "service to communities." In addition, it was happenstance that Ramsey's appeal for a deferment was rejected by his draft board, leading to his eventual involvement in radiation studies and work. It was circumstance that president Johnson would declare a "war on poverty" and initiate a drive to encourage service projects with communities.

Then there was even greater "chance" when Ramsay met Bob Sigmon. His brother, Dick, had a colleague that he thought might help Bill with his service project. Of course, that colleague was none other than Bob Sigmon, who had worked with the American Friends Service Committee and been a volunteer in Pakistan for several years. Sigmon claims he learned about the importance of "listening" to community members from that experience; which helped him shape the concept of doing service with community; something he called service learning. Had Ramsay's brother not known Bob Sigmon, who knows what this field would be called?

The tales of happenstance and happening, chance occurrences and the "dance" continue through almost everyone's stories. Tim Stanton discussed his life experiences, which were major framers of his involvement in service learning. He shares his early high school experience where his English teacher "grabbed him and a few other students" and involved them in a Civil Rights march in Connecticut. He doesn't recall how it happened, but relates the follow-up activities where he and his friends started a Civil Rights club, hoping to raise awareness of civil rights and social issues. He wanted to change things; and said that urge continues through today.

Then he worked one summer in an airplane engine parts manufacturing company and learned about the plight of blue collar factory workers. He hadn't known about these issues from his high school education. He joined the United Auto Workers and started his life work with the realization that the most important educational experiences "occurred outside" his traditional schooling. It sensitized him to the value of learning from community experiences and led to his passion to change the educational system.

His journey of happenstance was further developed when his freshman writing faculty at Stanford rejected his effort to connect his UAW experience with understanding the challenges in society. He was appalled that his teacher told him "his topic was not appropriate for an academic essay." He clearly felt otherwise, and vowed to work to be able to have academic experiences connect with issues and challenges in the real world.

His later experiences, working with Dwight Giles and others at Cornell University, developing and reporting about the great program they had developed, led to his continued efforts to connect with people and colleagues to pursue service learning around the country. His impact, from his work with Stanford President Donald Kennedy, to his efforts with Campus

Compact, made a noticeable difference. Tim used a variety of "happenstance occurrances" to truly make things happen for the field, for the country, and for the world.

This theme is repeated time and time again. Cathy Kaye tells of early experiences with her school in Maine where she "stumbled" into service learning by being fortunate enough to work with two remarkable educators, Mabel and George Dennison. These two individuals shared their wisdom and experience and made her aware of the importance of "listening to the children." These mentors, and the chance occurence of "elm disease" helped her to understand the importance of addressing real community problems. They helped shape her educational philosophy and practice, and provided a life-changing experience that propelled her to become one of the leading consultants in the world on service-learning pedagogy and practice.

Jane Permaul tells of her first connections by working with cooperative education efforts in Los Angeles. Her focus was on helping veterans from the Vietnamese War find suitable housing and employment, as result of the efforts of a California senator to provide such support and an initiative by the Reagan administration to close down mental health facilities in the country. A federal intiative, University Year for Action, was developed to support services to address community problems, including those of the mental health world. UCLA received funding to engage students in helping to settle displaced veterans in community group homes, and Jane learned of the great value that this experience had on helping college students to understand the problems in the community and how it could affect their college learning experience. So, the happenstance of the Vietnam War, a creative senator, disruptive federal policy, and a monetary grant all propelled Jane into the world of service, learning, and true university/community collaboration.

Terry Pickeral shared his story about being brought up in a home that valued/practiced service from an early age. His parents valued doing service with others and Terry considered it part of his DNA. He also learned to value the service that was provided to him when his father passed away at an early age. Terry went on to develop a program for at-risk teens in 1989. They worked with environmental projects and teachers taught him about the ability to connect academic subjects with the service activities. So, the happenstance of family roots, a family experience with service, and a school project where people taught him about the value of service and learning all propelled Terry along a lifetime of developing and promoting service-learning initiatives at all levels of education.

Jim Kielsmeier shared his story about being in the Army in South Korea and stumbling upon the opportunity to connect troops with students in Korean schools to help them learn English. Kielsmeier was challenged by a situation where South Koreans disliked Americans and was tasked to help change the attitudes of the occupying American troops and their South Korean hosts. He first tried lecturing the troops, hoping to convince them to alter their attitudes. When that didn't work, he collaborated with a colleague from the Korean army to develop a project to engage American troops as tutors in 14 middle and high schools. He had Peace Corps volunteers conduct the training. Troops volunteered in droves and things worked out very well. The project was very successful, with the Korean press praising the English Language Assistance Program, which was shared all over Korea. The army embraced it and Kielsmeier's doubting superior wrote the letter for his Army Commendation Medal. Who would have thought the Korean War would have had such an incredible impact on service learning in America as Kielsmeier went on to promote and develop some of the most important legislation, policy, and trainings for the United States and countries around the world.

And Bobby Hackett tells about his good fortune of being born into the right family at the right time. His father was already involved in and intimately connected to the Kennedy/Johnson initiatives around the war on poverty. Hackett's dad helped develop some of the early programs that led to many volunteer efforts, including Volunteers in Service to America (VISTA). Bobby interned with his father when he was in tenth grade, built a bookshelf in the basement of the Youth Policy Institute, and started learning how to do research to support service efforts. He was doing service learning long before he heard the term.

He went on to Harvard where he met, by chance, a student a few years ahead of him, Wayne Meisel. Wayne had the idea of organizing youth community service programs, including the first youth soccer league in Cambridge, Massachusetts. Using the framework of the old YMCA programs, Wayne decided to create a national organization to promote service, the Campus Outreach Opportunity League. How COOL was that!!!

Together, Bobby and Wayne went on to promote service and service-learning programs around the country. They connected with the National Society for Internships and Experiential Education (which was developing some of the early work on service learning) and collaborated with Campus Compact, which was formed around the same time as COOL.

The rest is history. Wayne went on to continue his work in the volunteer world and Bobby helped develop the Bonner Foundation, an entity committed to promoting the knowledge and skills of college students to serve as community change agents committed to social justice. So, the war on poverty and some lucky connections helped propel people, especially young people, into the world of service and service learning.

THE FUTURE

So, there you have it. The stories of people involved in service learning place the origins of the field in areas related to nuclear energy, the Vietnam War, the Korean War, the war on poverty, the civil rights movement, the simple experiences of young people being exposed to committed/insightful adults, and a history of personal and organizational collaborations that crossed the country and connected people, young and old, to a movement called service learning. There was no master plan. Only a series of chance occurances that connected people with a feel and sense of what it means to serve others and to learn from those service experiences. The experiences happend in a variety of places: schools, colleges, communities, homes, and families. And they happened because people had opportunities to do something, and had people and groups who helped them to develop and refine their knowledge and skills. It didn't happen on it's own. It happened because people were presented with opportunities, and they took those opportunities to make something happen. From happenstance to happening.

What can we learn from these stories and lessons that can inform our work for the next 40 years? What needs to be done to ensure that more and more people both do service learning and promote/expand its existence so that it becomes a normal part of growing up and developing into an engaged citizen? It seems the lessons learned from our leaders can be formalized and generalized into the following actions:

1. Don't worry; there will be new Bob Sigmons, Jane Permauls, Jim Kielsmeiers, and all the rest; it seems they develop naturally. There will be parents like Bobby Hackett's, teachers like those that influenced Cathy Kaye, and mentors like Bill Ramsay, who will continue to develop new people and expose them to elements of service learning.
2. Create similar environments for young people, from elementary school through college, and from community-based organizations to social clubs and social systems, to allow them to experience the opportunity to do service and to connect learning with the service. Clearly, schools, colleges, and out-of-school environments should be modeling the opportunities for children and youth to experience service and learning activities as part of their youth development. From school-based programs, to community-based organizations, having experiences like Tim Stanton, Bob Sigmon, and Bobby Hackett are necessary to instill in them the affect and practice of doing service learning. We need to ensure that such opportunities are not simply left to chance and happenstance; they can be modeled and molded so that every young person can sense

and taste the feelings of doing things for others and learning from those experiences.

3. Ensure that professional development opportunities are available for teachers, youth leaders, college faculty, and community members so they all can learn the policies, practicies, and problems of engaging in community connected learning and community connected service. This means teacher education programs, faculty development efforts, and comunity leader trainings all need to include lessons and activities that introduce people to the theories and practice of community engagement for service, for learning, and for social change.

4. Continue organizations, conferences, and meetings that bring people together who are doing service learning so they can connect and support others to improve their practice and provide the social networks and relationships that will build and expand the service-learning world. Some of the early practitioners and researchers felt isolated and somewhat removed from mainstream efforts. There is no longer a reason to have people feel this way when there are so many organizations, groups, and people who are doing it and can support others who want to learn and develop their practice. The world is better prepared for such experiential learning programs today than it was 40 years ago; so take advantage of the increased mass necessary for the movement to grow.

5. As Bobby Hackett learned from his dad, and others learned from their peers, conducting research and evaluation on the theories and practices of service learning is a necessary part of promoting the field. Feedback from participants, from community members, from organizations and institutions, and from policy/political actors is necessary to continue to propel the field forward. Service-learning efforts are not high quality unless they have evidence that service is being provided, learning is occuring for all involved, and social change is happening as a result. Research and evaluation are a critical element; and as many of our authors report, it helped them to grow in confidence that service learning is a legitimate, effective educational strategy and pedagogy.

6. Continue to focus on issues/problems that present themselves to humanity. Just as the nuclear energy issue of Bill Ramsay, the civil rights issues of John Duley, Tim Stanton, and Jane Permaul, the social justice issues of Bobby Hackett and Bob Sigmon, the school quality issues of Terry Pickeral and Rob Shumer, and the challenges of war and peace experienced by Jim Kielsmeier were motivators for these individuals, the problems faced by our nation and the world, such as health care, climate change, aging populations,

renewable energy, world peace, and feeding all the world's people can and will be great subjects for future service-learning practitioners. Social problems and adversity were the issues of the early practitioners. We need to continue to focus on making the world and our local communities a better place for everyone. Service-learning can be one of the major vehicles for making positive change happen.

We end here with a word that we started with: happen. Our original premise was that the authors who reported in this book went from happenstance to happening. They took chance opportunities and made something happen that was positive, was impactful, and helped shape the world of service learning and community connected civic education. While this early period of program/field development occurred by chance, it is anticipated that the next 40 years or so will move from chance occurrences to more intentionally developed experiences, where people who have worked in the service-learning world will provide guidance and support for the newcomers and those who continue to improve and refine their practice. The result of the last 40 years is a building of the mass of the movement; of assembling a large number of people who have come to know and do service learning in their personal and professional lives, and have joined together to create a field that is filled with enthusiastic, skilled, and knowledgeable people who can pass on their learning to future beneficiaries.

Despite the recent setbacks with the funding/guidance loss of the Corporation for National and Community Service and a few other funders, there is still strong interest in developing service learning in the United States and around the world. The challenges and needs of communities and societies throughout the world still require that people attempt to ensure that our values of service and communal work for social justice and social improvement will continue to be a strong driving force for education and social change. Hopefully, the stories and wisdom shared in this book will provide others with the inspiration, the insight, and the energy to continue the work of making the world a better place. That is a goal worthy of our best thinking and doing.

ABOUT THE EDITOR

Dr. Robert Shumer has been involved in education for almost 50 years. He has taught from middle school through graduate school and conducted research in many areas, from service learning, to teacher education, to character education, to career and technical education, to civic engagement, to participatory evaluation. He served as the founding director of the National Service-Learning Clearinghouse at the University of Minnesota and internal evaluator for the National Research Center for Career and Technical Education (NRCCTE). He also served as Director of Field Studies at UCLA and Vice Chair of the International Association for Research on Service Learning and Community Engagement. He has served on boards of directors for the National Society for Internships and Experiential Education, the International Association for Research on Service-Learning and Community Engagement, the National Youth Leadership Council, the American Red Cross, and the YMCA. He has published more than 85 articles, book chapters, and even a few books on service learning, youth-led participatory evaluation, career and technical education, teacher education, and community-based learning. He has also taught courses and consulted in many countries around the world, including Mexico, Germany, England, Ireland, Morocco, Canada, Japan, Taiwan, Singapore, and China.

He received his Masters in Educational Psychology from California State University, Northridge, and his PhD in Education from the University of California, Los Angeles (UCLA).

Where's the Wisdom in Service-Learning?, page 179
Copyright © 2017 by Information Age Publishing
All rights of reproduction in any form reserved.

CPSIA information can be obtained
at www.ICGtesting.com
Printed in the USA
LVOW13*1557200517

535184LV00006B/61/P